The 20 British Prime Ministers
of the 20th century

BONAR LAW

ANDREW TAYLOR

HAUS PUBLISHING • LONDON

First published in Great Britain in 2006 by
Haus Publishing Limited
26 Cadogan Court
Draycott Avenue
London SW3 3BX

www.hauspublishing.co.uk

A CIP catalogue record for this book is available from the British Library

ISBN 1-904950-59-0

Designed by BrillDesign
Typeset in Garamond 3 by MacGuru Ltd
info@macguru.org.uk

Printed and bound by Graphicom, Vicenza

Front cover: John Holder

Contents

Part One

THE LIFE

Chapter 1: Background

Andrew Bonar Law became Prime Minister at the age of 64 on 23 October 1922. On 19 May 1923, diagnosed with inoperable throat cancer, Law resigned, dying on 30 October. He was Prime Minister for only 209 days. Hence *The Unknown Prime Minister*, the title of Blake's biography. Law's career coincides with the emergence of modern British politics. He entered Parliament in 1900 and left it in 1923, for over half of this period (13 November 1911 to 21 March 1921 and 23 October 1922 to 28 May 1923) he was leader of the Conservative Party. Between December 1916 and March 1921, when he first retired from politics, he was *de facto* Deputy Prime Minister, as well as Chancellor of the Exchequer and Leader of the House. He was instrumental in destroying two prime ministers, Asquith and Lloyd George. In these 23 years Law confronted the rise of socialism, the advent of the welfare state, the onset of Britain's relative economic decline, the beginning of the break-up of the Empire, and the rise of the modern state. As Conservative leader he oversaw the party's modernisation, laying the foundations of Conservative hegemony between 1924 and 1964.

Prime ministers 'have come not from the ranks of the extrovert, the equable and the easy-going but from the introspective, the moody and the hypersensitive. Our most eminent political leaders have been distinguished, to an exceptional degree, by childhood bereavement and personal isolation'.[1] This could have been written with Law in mind. He was born on 16 September 1858 in his father's manse at Kingston in New Brunswick, Canada. The Revd. James Law was a Presbyterian minister of the Free Church of Scotland; he was born in Ulster and died in Ulster. Law's elder brother was to practise medicine there and Ulster was central to Bonar Law's political life. Law's mother, Annie (née Kidston, a Glaswegian banking family), who emigrated to Canada, died in 1860. Janet Kidston, Annie's sister, came out to look after the Revd. Law and his young family. When James remarried Janet decided to return to Scotland and offered to take Andrew, oversee his education and provide him with a business career in the family bank. The Revd. Law agreed, and Andrew left New Brunswick for Glasgow. There is uncertainty when he left Canada, 1865 or 1870, and whether he retained traces of his Canadian accent in adult life but Law was for all practical purposes, a scion of the solid, prosperous, professional Glaswegian bourgeoisie.

After preparatory school he attended Glasgow High School. He was an intelligent and hard-working boy and the Kidstons were wealthy enough to send him to Eton or Harrow, so they clearly took a decision not to do so. He left school at 16 and joined the family merchant bank. The Kidstons, three brothers and a sister, were childless and Law was heir to their fortune. Unlike the majority of the Glasgow commercial and industrial bourgeoisie who were Liberal in politics, the Kidstons were staunch Conservatives. Not only was Law exposed to Conservative politics in the home, he also met many leading Conservatives, so not surprisingly he gravitated to the Conservative Party. Law cannot be described as a 'doctrinal' in his politics. Personally cautious and pessimistic, these traits transferred into his politics but he was attracted to Conservative imperialism, 'the creed of the successful industrialists, of the engineers and technicians who were opening up a new world by their enterprise and their not always over-scrupulous vigour'.[2] The archetypes were men like Joseph Chamberlain, Law's self-confessed hero, and Rudyard Kipling, who was to become a friend.

Late in life Law confessed that of all the offices he held the appointment that gave him most pleasure was being made a bookkeeper at Kidstons. In 1885 Kidstons merged with the Clydesdale Bank. Unattracted by banking and anxious to strike out on his own, Law secured a partnership with William Jacks & Co, a firm of metal brokers. Kidstons had been intimately involved in financing the iron and steel industry and William Jacks & Co. was a client. In 1885 the senior partner, William Jacks, offered Law a partnership. Bankrolled by the Kidstons, Law, at the age of 27, began his independent business career.

When Law joined William Jacks the Glasgow iron market was booming. Producers of pig iron lodged their output at Connals' Stores, which issued warrants entitling their owners to a quantity of iron. Iron merchants like Jacks were intermediaries between producers and consumers dealing in these warrants at the Royal Exchange. The 'iron ring' (literally, the merchants sat in a circle) met between 11–12 and 2–3, at the end of business warrants were exchanged and cash

The Glasgow iron ring was emblematic of late-Victorian capitalism, a microcosm of its strengths and weaknesses: profitable but unstable. A speculative trade subject to rapid fluctuation, the market was acutely sensitive to gossip and rumour, as well as external shocks. The iron market relied on the Scottish industry supplying large quantities of cheap iron but was facing growing competition from newer and cheaper producers in Cleveland utilising the new Bessemer technology, which could not be used on Scottish ores.

settlements made. As a market Glasgow was facing growing competition from London, the Empire's mercantile centre. Jacks diversified seeking new clients, including Krupps and the Nova Scotia Steel and Coal Company, and set up offices in Middlesborough and London. Jacks' Glasgow operation eventually failed and by the 1920s Law's holdings were virtually worthless.

By the 1890s Law was, through a combination of hard work, acumen and inheritance, enjoying an annual income of about £6,000. Though no bloated plutocrat, Law's wealth conferred independence. His social origins and business career are often portrayed as marking him out as a transitional figure in party history, symbolising the shift from landed to commercial wealth. Law made no secret that his politics had been influenced by his business career; *nobody knows better than I that political work cannot be done on strictly business lines but the nearer you can approach business lines the better for political work.*[3] Before 1914 one-third of the parliamentary party were businessmen and Law is often presented as their representative. He was not a manufacturer but a finance capitalist whose business career gave him a detailed knowledge of Britain's Imperial political economy.

Nobody knows better than I that political work cannot be done on strictly business lines but the nearer you can approach business lines the better for political work.

BONAR LAW

Law did not attend university. He was, however, a voracious reader of history (Carlyle and Gibbon's *The Decline and Fall of the Roman Empire* were favourites) and mystery stories and he attended early-morning lectures at Glasgow University before work. His autodidacticism was, like business, a means to an end: a political career. The Glasgow Parliamentary Debating Association, of which Law was an active member for a decade, modelled itself on the House of Commons' procedures. It conducted debates under a Speaker and published a 'Hansard'; it passed bills, it had a Prime Minister, ministers and a Leader of the Opposition and its members represented constituencies (Law's was North Staffordshire). Here, and as a spectator in the bankruptcy court, Law developed and honed his rhetorical skills and his biographers see the Association as Law's Oxford Union, which prepared him for the House of Commons.

In March 1891 Law married Annie Pitcairn Robley. Law was clearly smitten with Annie; in his pursuit of her he even attended balls and fancy dress parties. Law profoundly disliked music and the theatre; he was utterly ignorant of and indifferent to hunting, shooting and fishing, and attended country house parties only for political reasons. This was a happy and fulfilling marriage, which produced five children, one of which was stillborn, and Law and Annie were devoted to each other. Law was not gregarious but he was an involved and even indulgent father who clearly enjoyed all aspects family life. Law's table and cellar were legendary in the party (meat and vegetables [boiled] followed by rice pudding figure prominently) and his colleagues strove to avoid them. He was also teetotal, preferring cordials or ginger ale, out of dislike of alcohol rather than principle, although his elder brother was an alcoholic. Tom Jones, the assistant Cabinet Secretary, noted Law's needs were simpler than even Lloyd George's, and having gobbled his two courses indulged his passion for tobacco, a passion that eventually killed him.

Law is invariably described as gloomy and melancholic. This may have been inherited from his father and, like Winston Churchill and Harold Macmillan, he was subject to 'the black dog'. Law had good grounds to be depressed. On the other hand, many commented approvingly on Law's self-deprecating sense of humour and mordant, dry wit. Soon after his election as leader the initially sceptical Chief Whip described Law as 'charming to deal with – most thoughtful and kind, melancholy in disposition, witty when moments of relaxation occur, devoted to his family, profoundly convinced of the justice of his case. With an unerring memory, much courage, greater resources and industry he ought to go far.'[4]

Despite his dislike of socialising, not only did Law enjoy good company, he *was* good company. Lloyd George, not one to waste his time with dullards, came to regard Law with great affection and enjoyed spending time with him. LG's mistress noted 'Since Bonar left he has lost an ideal companion with whom he could laugh & joke and enjoy himself.' Despite, or perhaps because of, his upbringing Law had no discernible religious beliefs. At a service at St Margaret's Westminster Willie Bridgeman 'saw Bonar reading the Te Deum … as if he had never seen it before'. Reflecting on Law's funeral Tom Jones believed, 'All these prayers and hymn singing very alien to the B.L. known to me. He once remarked to me that L.G. still had some sort of a belief in a future life and clearly implied to me that that he, B.L. had none whatever.'[5] Max Aitken, later Lord Beaverbrook, a very close friend, described him as 'unassuming'; 'His personality stamped itself in no way upon the casual acquaintance … he was quite indifferent to the opinion which outsiders might form of him. In his immediate circle, he was most anxious to make himself agreeable and could wield great charm.'[6] Maynard Keynes, who worked with Law at the Treasury during the war, wrote that Law's 'modest, gentle, unselfish ways have won for him affection from all who have worked near him'.[7]

Law's dourness gave little clue to his 'hinterland'. He was a keen golfer, spoke passable French and German and his tennis style was like his politics: vigorous and difficult to counter. Law enjoyed billiards, bridge and, above all, chess. When commuting in Glasgow he would play or solve chess problems. Experts regarded him as a good player but inclined to recklessness and Law described chess as *a cold bath for the mind.* Few expert chess players are good politicians and few good politicians are chess adepts but politics and chess have common qualities. Good chess players and effective politicians have the ability to see further into the game than their opponents and an appreciation of the importance of manoeuvre, of attack and defence, and of sacrifice for a greater gain. One of Law's favourite opening gambits was 'the Spanish torture', or 'Spanish opening', invented by Ruy Lopez, a 16th-century priest, who advocated placing the board so the sun shone in the opponent's eyes. It is called the Spanish torture because White, if he knows how, can torment his opponent. White attacks the Knight defending the e-pawn so black either defends the e-pawn or exchanges it so surrendering the centre of the board. Keynes drew a direct connection between politics and chess and how Law's mind worked. Law assumed that 'the pieces on the board constituted the whole premises of the argument, that any attempt to look too far ahead was too hypothetical and difficult to be worthwhile, and that one was playing the game in question *in vacuo*, with no ulterior purpose except to make the right move in that particular game'.[8] This attribute led to accusations of excessive caution, which 'leads him when coming to a decision to cast his mind twelve months forward in order to picture to himself the probable retrospect'.[9] This approach underpinned Law's reputation for common sense, candour and integrity. It also disguised his cunning. Law was never as simple as he looked.

In 1897 Law began his search for a constituency. In 1898 he was adopted for the Glasgow constituency of Blackfriars and Hutchestown. This had been Liberal since 1884 and the sitting MP, A D Provand, a Manchester merchant, was a popular figure. Law recognised it would not be easy to wrest the seat from the Liberals and probably did not expect to win. Nevertheless, he campaigned hard and proved an accomplished speaker with a formidable memory; he also demonstrated he could use language to draw blood. At the age of 42 Law won Blackfriars and Hutchestown with the help of the 1900 'Khaki' election, but there was little doubt that his own qualities persuaded many voters.

Law immediately wound up his business activities, while retaining his directorships. Accustomed to the cut and thrust of the iron-ring, Law, as the lowest form of parliamentary life – the new backbencher – initially found Parliament staid and unfulfilling. Austen Chamberlain recalled a disconsolate Law saying, *'it was all very well for men who, like myself had been able to enter the House of Commons young to adapt to a Parliamentary career, but that if he had known what the House of Commons was he would never have entered at this stage'*.[10] Two weeks later Law delivered his maiden speech in response to Lloyd George's attack on the government's conduct of the South African War. Although his speech attracted no public notice, his peers thought he had done well and noted Law's willingness to bare his teeth in debate.

In late-Victorian politics Irish Home Rule, Britain's place in the world and the emerging 'social question' were intertwined. As the party of national unity and Empire the party could not insulate itself from these issues. At the eye of this developing storm was Joe Chamberlain. Splitting with Gladstone over Home Rule with his interest in social reform undimmed meant this mercurial figure both attracted and repelled Conservatives. After 1895 Chamberlain drew closer to the Conservatives. Stimulated by his interest in empire, Chamberlain evolved his 'grand unifying theory' of politics. Imperial political, economic and military integration would enable the Empire to compete globally with the United States and Imperial Germany, would provide cheap raw materials and guaranteed markets for Britain's manufacturers so securing working class prosperity and political acquiescence. Chamberlain's vision clashed with free trade, the political-economic orthodoxy since Peel's repeal of the Corn Laws. For many politicians and voters free trade was the political Ark of the Covenant, the secret of domestic prosperity, and tariff reform challenged this orthodoxy. Law, as a self-made businessman, was intimately acquainted with the late-Victorian imperial political economy and was drawn to Chamberlain. Though not an enthusiast for Chamberlain's social politics, his identification with Chamberlain aided Law's career, leading to his appointment on 8 August 1902 as parliamentary secretary to the Board of Trade. He had his foot on the first rung. Law lost his seat in the 1906 landslide but his worth to the party was demonstrated when he was quickly found a seat at Dulwich. Despite the party's defeat, Law could afford to be optimistic. He had no money worries; he enjoyed a happy and secure home life and had enjoyed a rapid rise. Law cultivated a reputation as a party man, effective in debate and trusted by his leaders and colleagues. He looked forward to preferment in the next Conservative government.

On 31 October 1909 Law's wife died suddenly after a gall bladder operation. He was devastated. Law never really recovered from his wife's death and it was especially profound for a man already prone to melancholia, who could not console himself with religion. J C C Davidson, who became Law's secretary in 1916, believed he 'always had a feeling that he had neglected her – not that that had led to her illness, but he felt that he hadn't paid nearly enough attention to her or to his family. It had a tremendous effect on his life, because he was always melancholy with the thought that he should have been less selfish.'[11]

This proved a turning point and politics saved him. Widowhood brought two people into his intimate circle that were to have great significance. The first was his sister, Mary Law. Mary became his châtelaine, looking after his home and children but she was also important in his political life. Davidson recognised her significance, using Aunt Mary as 'back channel'. Davidson and Aunt Mary discussed issues and 'I used to persuade her, and having persuaded her, she would go to Bonar and say: "You can't do that." I used Aunt May to do things or not to do things almost at will, because Aunt Mary could get him to do almost anything.'[12] Mary Law was a formidable woman. With a strong character, her intelligence and loyalty enabled her to discuss politics with Law (and vice-versa) but no one manipulated Law and he was well aware of Davidson's indirect strategy. Davidson, for example, was unable to use Aunt Mary, who like Davidson, disliked Lloyd George, to persuade Law not to ally with him in December 1916. Mary Law made it clear that she would provide the domestic support to Law's public career but would not play any social role. Socialising at high politics held no attraction, but this did not affect his career. Withdrawal helped Law cultivate the image of a serious politician.

The second was Max Aitken, later Lord Beaverbrook. Law and Aitken had been doing business since 1908 but they were brought closer together by Edward Goulding, then MP for Worcester, later Lord Wargrave, and a wealthy City financier. The friendship between Aitken and Law took some time to flourish. Aitken saw in Law a fellow New Brunswicker, businessman and, most important, a coming man who could help his entry into British politics and Law helped Aitken secure the Ashton-under-Lyne constituency. Law's connection with Aitken's circle did not arouse universal enthusiasm. Aunt Mary, for example, initially disliked Aitken but came to recognise his value to her brother. More seriously, party grandees feared Aitken's influence when Law became party leader in 1911.[13] Law bitterly resented interference with his friendships. He was aware of Aitken's dubious reputation as a political and financial manipulator; this did not deter Law, who regarded Aitken as a sounding board, source of information and a diversion. Law listened to Aitken's advice but did not always follow it. He did discuss highly sensitive politics with Aitken but never revealed state secrets and 'their relationship was extremely personal and very cordial [but] he knew his Max ... there was absolutely no corruption in his relationship with Bonar Law, to who he had an extraordinary devotion'.[14]

When he became leader some Conservatives thought Law a 'slacker'. Law's confidence soon grew and *'after a long period of depression ... is rapidly emerging a greater man from despondency. Certainly the atmosphere of Pembroke Lodge, the widower's home, is wan, cheerless, dejected. Perhaps ... this interval has made him a statesman'.*[15] His wife's death pulled Law deeper into politics: 'from this point [he] regarded his political career not only as a demanding task of national importance, but as an antidote to what sometimes seemed unutterable loneliness.'[16]

'From this point [Law] regarded his political career not only as a demanding task of national importance, but as an antidote to what sometimes seemed unutterable loneliness.'

R J Q ADAMS

Law remained an isolated figure and two further deaths deepened Law's melancholia. On 19 April 1917 Charlie Law, his second son who was serving in the 3rd Battalion King's Own Scottish Borderers, was reported missing at the second

Battle of Gaza. Law hoped that his son had been taken prisoner by the Turks but Charlie was dead. In September, James, his eldest son and an RFC pilot, was transferred at his own request to a fighter squadron in France. He was shot down on 21 September. Visiting his son's squadron Law sat for two hours in the cockpit of a machine of the type flown by his son. The saddest thing for a parent is to bury a child. Law did not have this consolation as Charlie was buried in Palestine and James' body was never identified. Law, like so many others, found the strength to go on but the death of his two sons changed him. 'The war,' Baldwin recalled, 'brought him high office and great power, but these rewards were no consolation. By the end he cared neither for office nor for politics. Only a sense of duty and perhaps the anodyne which hard work gave to his wounds kept him still in public life.' Law, like many, 'was changed by the war' and, recalling his love of family, Baldwin believed he 'probably he never recovered from the loss of his wife ... From the loss of the boys ... he certainly never recovered.'[17] Rudyard Kipling, a friend of both Law and Baldwin, who lost his only son at the Battle of Loos, wrote a series of *Epitaphs of the War*, two of which, *A Grave Near Cairo* and *R.A.F (Aged Eighteen)*, convey some sense of Law's desolation. A third, *A Dead Statesman,* articulates the guilt that political class might have felt. Kipling wrote, 'And I must face the men I slew. / What tale shall serve me here among/ Mine angry and defrauded young?' Did these lines speak to Law? A political career is always costly, Law's was costlier than most: 'If it is lonely at the top, it is because it is the lonely who seek to climb there.'[18]

Blake suggests Law lacked the killer instinct, 'that happy gift ... the ability to take a hard and ruthless decision, and carry it through without further doubts or qualms of conscience.'[19] This confuses Law's melancholia and tendency to brood with indecision, for which he was often criticised. In 1916 during the conscription crisis, for example, Lloyd George, after dining with Law, confessed 'he has never seen anyone in such a state of abject funk ... [BL] does not know which way to turn or what to do.' In the November crisis LG described Law as the 'only weak spot ... [He] cannot make up his mind to strike'; and in 1918, Amery commented acidly, 'Bonar showed himself more than usually terrified about any sort of decision.' Selbourne liked Law but thought him a poor leader who 'lacks vision, initiative and driving power; I am afraid he also lacks courage; he only once in my time took any strong line ... generally he gave the impression to the Cabinet that he was an amateur in politics.' [20]

Law's indecision was an aversion to precipitate action, which, he believed, could do more harm than good. His experience was that in Conservative politics divisive issues could escalate easily, whereas vagueness could, with an emphasis on maximising the common ground, steer the party into calmer waters. Imprecision could wrong-foot opponents, increasing his room for manoeuvre. The result was 'a paradoxical combination of diffidence and decision' and Salisbury felt 'there was a good deal of Launcelot Gobbo in him ... a courageous and shrinking Bonar Law, wrestling with one another all the time'. [21] Acutely sensitive to charges of bad faith, dishonourable conduct and opportunism, Law was 'capable of occasional flashes of personal ambition, which blazed out in the face of critical opposition from supporters or colleagues or of abuse in the public Press.' The infrequency of his anger and its contrast with Law's usual demeanour demonstrated a line had been drawn. Beaverbrook felt Law's lack of self-interest made him a patriot but to say 'he fell short of greatness' because he lacked the capacity 'to be ruthless for the public good'. This is nonsense. [22]

Law was not ruthless in the sense of being devoid of pity or compassion but he could be implacable and remorseless. A J P Taylor describes him as 'the most formidable giant-killer of the century'.[23] Without these qualities he could not have become or have remained party leader in this turbulent period and could not have broken Asquith and Lloyd George. Law strove to make the relationship with Asquith and the Coalition work but: 'Once he was convinced that it was impossible for it to do so, however, he destroyed it almost without a second thought.'[24] A common mistake is to assume a politician's ability to detach him or herself reveals a basic indifference and lack of a killer instinct rather than a strategic ability to appraise a situation clinically. As Machiavelli advocated in *The Prince*, Law combined the fox and the lion: 'one must be a fox in order to recognise traps, and a lion to frighten off wolves. Those who simply act like lions are stupid.' Law was not stupid.

Chapter 2: The Rise of a Good Party Man

Law placed tremendous emphasis on rhetoric. Before mass electronic communication, politicians saw the speech as an instrument of articulation and persuasion. Speeches were also personally important: 'The road to political honour twists its way along the floor of Parliament ... There is the pleasure of having stirred, or impressed or entertained an audience, and the gratification which accrues on having exposed and discredited an adversary.'[1]

Law seldom used notes and never a script; he had no speechwriter although one of Davidson's tasks was to revise Law's speeches for Hansard because he tended to leave out the verbs. Law preferred to compose his speeches sitting quietly for hours, working his speech through in his mind and then relying on his prodigious memory. Law was not a florid speaker but strove to express what his audience was thinking. Even for politicians of this era Law was 'addicted to pure debate'. 'His mind,' the Chief Whip wrote, 'is strict and precise in logic, the construction of his argument seems based on a geometrical thesis, his whole style is that of a keen logician who desires the issues settled upon the merits of the argument.'[2] Time pressures meant that as party leader he spent less time working on his speeches and making greater use of intuition and reading his audience. In 1906 Leo Amery describe one of his speeches as 'First rate' contrasting Law's

with F E Smith's 'vigorous but unfinished effort'.[3] Law was difficult to handle in debate:

'He was a heaven-sent debater because by the time his opponents had decided what they were going to say and were about to interrupt him or ask a question, the time had flown by and he was half-way through the next subject. He never bothered to finish a sentence when he had made his point and saw that the House had obviously grasped what he was getting at.'[4]

Law grew to political maturity in a culture – political and parliamentary – that valued the spoken word. In Glasgow Law had single-mindedly learned how to be heard in that culture. Friend and foe alike appreciated his oratorical and rhetorical skills. Law learned how to hold and persuade an audience, an audience which, he knew, would be lost if they did not like his message.

A political culture oriented around the spoken word rewarded those who could exploit the opportunities it offered and Law devoted enormous effort developing the necessary skills to exploit this culture. Law's era was also the era of the rise of the popular press. This pointed to a decline in the spoken word's saliency but newspapers still reported speeches verbatim and Law was well aware of this. Law made great efforts to ensure that his speeches read as he wanted them to be read, which is why he revised his method of formulating speeches. Rhetoricians identify two types of audience: the real and the ideal. The real audience can respond to words – the House of Commons or the public platform – whereas the ideal audience – the mass readership of the new popular press – does not speak back. In late 19th and early 20th century political culture there was an emerging tension between speaking and reading and Law, like Lloyd George, operated at the cusp of a new era of mass political communication. In rhetorical terms this was the decisive shift from a real to an ideal audience. Contemporaries noted this change. Noting that Law was 'making himself feared' in the House, the Chief Whip contrasted Law with Balfour: 'Whereas A.J.B. was adored in parliament, he failed to strike the imagination or to fire the zeal of our supporters outside and in the constituencies. With B.L. the exact reverse will hold good.'[5] For Law's approach to work his speeches had to influence the ideal and the real, and after Law politicians increasingly focussed on the ideal audience.

Law's style was the product of a tension between caution, diffidence and aggression. Law would think long and hard about a course of action but once he had decided he would push on to the end. Law was also aware of the value of political theatre. This was reflected in his language but also in various tricks. Thus, 'his suits were made with a number of hidden pockets, and in the heat of debate he would sometimes reach into one to extract a small notebook or scrap of paper ... few knew that the papers were often unimportant or even blank.'[6] The party leadership forced changes: 'his method of committing every speech to memory is cumbersome ... he will have to speak so often and on such varied

> Arthur James Balfour (1848–1930) had succeeded his uncle Lord Salisbury as Conservative Party leader and Prime Minister in 1902, but was decisively defeated by the Liberals in the general election of 1905. He remained as party leader until replaced by Bonar Law in 1911, but continued to play a part in politics, serving as First Lord of the Admiralty in Asquith's wartime coalition, and then as Foreign Secretary under Lloyd George, issuing the famous Balfour Declaration in 1917 recognising a Jewish 'national home' in Palestine, and became Lord President of the Council under Baldwin in 1925. (See *Balfour* by Ewen Green, in this series.)

topics that ample preparation will no longer be feasible.'
There were other changes: 'with real reluctance he feels that
the world is not governed by the reasonable marshalling of
fact and figure before an impartial jury – and he is driven to
employ the bludgeon as well as the rapier.'[7]

Comparing Law's rhetoric to the hammering of rivets in a
Glasgow shipyard is amusing but it was held responsible for
a heightened confrontation and increased vitriol in politics.
'The New Style' was widely criticised as a decline in civility
but any decline, if decline there was, could be plausibly dated
from Lloyd George's 1909 Limehouse Declaration and his
goading of the House of Lords. Under Law the Chief Whip
detected a change of mood in a party hitherto 'disheartened by
the terrible paucity of numbers, by the overweening bearing
of our opponents, and by the galling sense of our own defeat'.[8]
Balfour appeared incapable of exploiting this new combative-
ness from MPs crying out for a lead. Despite the Conservative
gains in 1910 the brutal reality of the parliamentary arithmetic was, because of what Law described as Asquith's 'corrupt
bargain' with the Irish Nationalist MPs over Home Rule, the
government was secure.

'The New Style' received a very public airing during the
first reading of the Home Rule bill. Asquith suggested Law
would not repeat in the Commons comments made outside
about the government's indebtedness to the Irish Nationalists. Law insisted he would.

'The PRIME MINISTER: Am I to understand that the
right hon. Gentleman repeats here, or is prepared to repeat
on the floor of the House of Commons –

Mr BONAR LAW: Yes.

The PRIME MININSTER: Let us see exactly what it is: It
is that I and my colleagues are selling our convictions.

Mr BONAR LAW: You have not got any.

The PRIME MINISTER: We are getting on with the new style.'[9]

The flaccidity of Asquith's rejoinder indicates the astonishment Law's response caused. Law's own supporters were delighted. Balfour had been too accommodating to 'truculent and frequently insolent' Liberals. 'The Party,' the Chief Whip concluded, 'in its subconscious way, likes Bonar Law's attitude precisely because it lacks those very qualities which … conform to high parliamentary tradition.'[10] Lord Selbourne believed the party's failings after 1906 were 'a want of faith, a vacillation, an opportunism' which testified to 'shallow convictions and a want of moral courage'. However:

'When leaders such as you lead, the followers will end by following, and the new style "to say what you mean and mean what you say" is really supreme wisdom, because of its simplicity and because the moral courage which it connotes, and the greatest and rarest and most demonstrably greatest of all the political virtues is moral courage …'[11]

At the 1911 party conference, his first as leader, Law told his audience about some advice he had received on his election as leader, *that in the House of Commons in the future I should not be so rude* – (laughter) – *as I have been in the past. It is possibly good advice, and I shall at least remember it.* (Laughter). *But in the severe and, I am afraid, bitter fight which lies before us – a fight for everything we hold dear* – (cheers) – *I have really no hope of acting in such a way as to satisfy the giver of that advice.*[12] Pursuing this theme, Law asked Asquith; *Has it not occurred to the right hon. Gentleman that what is new is not the style of the criticism, but the things that have to be criticised when we are dealing with a new standard of decency?*[13]

In a febrile political climate, where political arithmetic rendered the Conservatives powerless, language was Law's only weapon. Language and rhetoric could be used to berate ministers, unite the party and direct its frustrations outward, and mobilise anti-Liberal and anti-Irish sentiment in preparation for the election. In his memoirs Asquith hints that Law's rhetoric was an artifice. At the 1912 State Opening of Parliament he reported Law's saying: *I am afraid I shall have to show myself very vicious, Mr Asquith, this session. I hope you will understand.*[14] Asquith is the only source for an imputation of insincerity that seems out of character. Rather than a semi-apology or a nod-and-a-wink from one professional to another this, if it was made, is an example not of Law's deviousness but his straightforwardness: he was making both a threat and a promise. If it was said, it flowed not from a cynical view of the political game but from a deep conviction that Asquith's government was a mortal threat to the Constitution. Ministers 'fear and dislike Bonar Law because he is unsparing in scathing denunciation'; the party liked Law 'because their attitude is uncompromising and because it conforms to their belief in his genuine distrust of the Radical Policy. His speeches help them to understand what they firmly believe, namely the utter lack of true public spirit which animates the Radical Party.'[15]

Law's rhetoric on Ulster has tended to obscure the fact that he 'was almost devoid of Conservative principles'. Law, had according to Keynes, 'no imaginative reverence for the traditions and symbols of the past, no special care for vested interests, no attachment whatever to the Upper Classes, the City, the Army, or the Church. He is prepared to consider each question on its merits.'[16] Law himself declared his freedom from dogma: *I am a Conservative, not merely in a party sense, but I think by temperament, and I like old forms when they have any meaning.*[17] Law's Conservatism 'proceeded from caution, scepticism, lack of faith, distrust of any intellectual process which proceeded more than one or two steps ahead, or any emotional enthusiasm which grasped at an intangible object, and an extreme respect for all kinds of *Success*.'[18] This conception of Conservatism was undogmatic but lacked neither beliefs or passion; 'Bonar Law is interested in subjects, not in politics.'[19] In mid-1907 Law was described as 'an able man, and a good speaker' but his manner and prestige 'could [only] lead a party for a few months with success'. The aristocratic Balcarres sensed resentment in the bourgeois Law, a feeling of being slighted and undervalued.[20] Four years later Law was party leader. Before this, however, he had to endure defeat and bereavement.

I am a Conservative, not merely in a party sense, but I think by temperament, and I like old forms when they have any meaning.

BONAR LAW

In January 1906 the Conservatives won 157 seats, the Liberals 401, the Irish Nationalists 83 and Labour 29. This cataclysm was the backdrop to Law's rise. Law believed he would find it difficult to hold his Glasgow seat. The Labour candidate, George H Barnes, an engineer and trade union official, defeated him by 310 votes. Barnes' defeat of Law captures the changing nature of British politics with the rise of Labour and expresses the changing balance of political forces facing Conservatives. Barnes held Blackfriars until 1918. Barnes' victory over Law seemed to confirm Balfour's conviction that the 1906 defeat was more than a 'swing of the pendulum, and inaugurated a new political era. 'We are,' Balfour believed, 'face to face (no doubt in a milder form) with the Socialist difficulties which loom large on the Continent.'[21]

That Law was an anti-Socialist is unremarkable. Condemning Lloyd George's budgets, Law lambasted Liberal ministers for prosecuting a class war – against certain categories of wealth (*wealth which has not been invested in land*) but wealthy Liberals were thereby digging their own political graves; *So long as these proposals apply to land their withers remain unwrung. But do they imagine that the proposals are going to stop at land?*[22] Pursuing a narrow short-term partisanship, the Liberals had opened the door to a general attack on property. Socialism was Utopian because it denied human nature, *private enterprise under equal conditions would always beat State enterprise. The motive lay in the mainsprings of human nature, that motive was personal energy, and it was based largely upon personal ambition. If they took away that they took away one of the strongest forces for progress.*[23] During the debates on Lloyd George's 1909 Budget, Law argued there were two types of socialism. *Ordinary Socialism*, he argued, *as far as politics are concerned, means creating and encouraging discontent and fostering cupidity. For all practical purposes Socialism as a political force means unjust taxation.*[24] Lloyd George and George Barnes were symptomatic of the new politics. The careers of Law and Barnes converged. Barnes was vice-chairman of the Parliamentary Labour Party (1908–10) and chair (1910–11) but after the outbreak of war in 1914 Barnes increasingly identified with 'patriotic labour' and became a leading member of the British Workers' League, later the National Democratic Labour Party (NDLP). Law was instrumental in encouraging patriotic labour in an effort to split the Labour vote in the Coalition's interest. Barnes and Law became colleagues under Lloyd George. Barnes resigned from the Labour Party in 1918 and as leader of the NDLP sat for Glasgow Gorbals until 1922.

His defeat in 1906, the Liberal–Labour alliance, and the pre-1914 industrial unrest raised the question of how the party should engage with the working class. Working class engagement with the war convinced Law that mass democracy could not be resisted and that the real threat was not democracy but socialism, the logical extension of democracy. The failure of Barnes and the NDLP made it clear that the Conservatives' main enemy was the Labour Party. This was in the future but for Law the Liberals' 1906 victory was the opening shot in a war that could destroy society. This was Law's first election defeat and it rankled. However, he was found a seat a Dulwich and returned to the Commons in May 1906. This speedy return reflected his good standing in the party and recognition that his talents were needed.

In 1908–09 Law developed a critique of the government that revolved around the charge that the Liberal government would do anything to retain office and that this governance was profoundly politically corrosive and morally degenerate. The 1908 budget, and other bills, was motivated by demagoguery appealing to the basest political motives. Income tax increases and death duties were to pay for old age pensions and Law thought it significant that ministers had ruled out a contributory scheme. The reliance on direct taxation marked the Liberals' shift from social reform to socialism.

The real and vital distinction for Law between legitimate social reform and practical Socialism was the method by which those reforms were to be paid for. If they were to be paid for by all classes of the community in proportion to their ability, then it was just and fair social reform. If, on the other hand, they were to be paid for entirely by one class exclusively for the benefit of another class, then it was practical Socialism.[25]

Confiscatory taxation damaged the economy and was a manifestation of class war. Liberals had two ways of securing electoral popularity. *The positive way,* Law argued, *is by bribing every class which they hope may possibly vote for them. The negative way is by punishing the classes which they are sure will vote against them*. Punishment of the aristocracy was Lloyd George's motivation, which demonstrated that class animosity and class war were fundamental to the government's programme.

Direct taxation would drive out capital and destroy incentives and by attacking property rights. Liberals were *making the security of property of every kind less than in any civilised country in the world.* Land taxes were the most significant politically because *they show clearly and unmistakably that we are face to face in this country for the first time, and I hope, so far as our lifetime is concerned, with a Socialist Budget.*[26]

Law was neither religious nor a member of the established church so he had no doctrinal concerns about church disestablishment, but disestablishment and disendowment of the Church of Wales encapsulated Law's disquiet about the interconnection between democracy, the threat to property, and the tyranny of the majority. Ministers argued that as Parliament had both established and endowed the Welsh church it could disestablish and disendow. This use of parliamentary sovereignty horrified Law. The Welsh church had obtained these funds by an Act of 1662, so stripping the church of its property after such a time *would shake to its foundations the whole security of property on which civilisation depends.* He continued, *I do not deny that Parliament has the power to take away that property. But Parliament has equally the right to take every farthing that the right hon. Gentleman has and give it to me. It is a power, but it is not a right ... it is confiscation.* Confiscation was legitimised by the democratic will: a majority of the Welsh people wanted this measure, so they must have it. The popular will was important but Parliament should not act merely because a majority willed it. Parliament was a representative, not delegatory, body and 500,000 people in Wales had signed petitions opposing the bill. What of their rights? Parliament, insulated from 'the majority', was the only legitimate decision-maker: *It is for us to decide whether or not it is right or just, and you have got to convince us that it is just.* Thus, under the Liberals' new politics, a long-established institution enshrined in the law and constitution, was to have its property stripped and redistributed by a parliamentary majority responding to what it interpreted as the popular will.[27]

The government's decision to impose new duties on Scottish and Irish spirits was bitterly criticised as unfair by Redmond and the Irish Nationalists. Law agreed the duties were unfair but Redmond could easily have them removed: *If he chooses to take off his coat he can be sure that this tax will either be taken off or greatly diminished.* The Liberals' commitment to Home Rule had joined the Irish to the government; the Irish would be betraying their country's interests by not resisting the duties because of the primacy they placed on Home Rule. Law criticised the Liberals for abandoning principles of sound finance for party advantage and indulging in electoral bribery, a tendency Law felt was inevitable in popular government. Democracy introduced a new political principle: *The new principle is to use the control of the finances of the country to win back the popularity which they have lost.* Old age pensions were the first manifestation but the shift to the new politics was now well underway because, *Into this Budget they have thrown haphazard every one of the extreme nostrums which have been current fair at Socialist meetings at street corners for years.*[28]

In the conflicts between tariff reformers and free traders Law was careful not to be identified with, for example, Amery's *Compatriots* or Henry Page Croft's *Confederates* but did join the Tariff Reform League's governing committee. Law was careful to do nothing that could be interpreted as challenging Balfour's leadership and he endorsed, albeit with reluctance, the tariff reformers' *Unauthorised Programme* published on 12 October 1908. This sought the maintenance of the Union with Ireland, tariff reform, tax reform, House of Lord reform, social reform and compulsory military service. Despite his association with the *Unauthorised Programme*, Law made his scepticism known to Fabian Ware, one of the programme's leading lights.[29] Joe Chamberlain's cerebral haemorrhage and retirement saw the tariff reform mantle passed to Austen but Law, who joined the Shadow Cabinet, did not need the Tariff Reform League as a vehicle. It was during this period that Law was clearly a 'coming man' and began to be spoken of as a future leader and a major asset in the battles with the Liberal government. He also ensured that he kept open links to all parts of the party.

Law had no problems fighting the Liberals and few doubted his sincerity but he knew that many tariff reformers doubted his adherence to the Chamberlainite programme. Equally, Law was aware that many Conservatives feared tariff reform would shatter the party, leaving the Church, the Constitution and the Union defenceless. Law attracted the Whips' suspicion and there were jibes that all his speeches, irrespective of topic, were always about tariff reform. Law had nothing to do with anti-Balfour plots and his caution seemed justified when, in November 1907, Balfour promulgated his policy of retaliatory tariffs. The Conservatives faced an insurmountable Liberal majority; the Liberals faced a similarly robust Conservative majority in the House of Lords. The Lords' veto gave the Conservatives a powerful weapon that, given the legislation emanating from the government, would inevitably be used. Law could expect to be called upon by the leadership and he recognised he could enhance his reputation in the parliamentary battles. He had nothing to gain from undermining Balfour. Law was a loyal party spokesman rather than a trusted adviser but was clearly a player in Conservative politics.

Faced by the Lords' veto of Lloyd George's 'People's Budget', Asquith called a general election for January 1910. The Liberals announced they would remove the veto, the last institutional obstacle to Home Rule. Edward VII, who died on 6 May 1910, had made it clear that before this happened he would wish to see a second election. As a result of the election the Lords passed the budget but it was too late. Asquith, now dependent on Redmond's Irish MPs, who made it clear that they would support the Liberal government in return for an override of the Lords' veto, was determined to destroy the Conservative's majority in the Lords. George V sponsored a six-month Constitutional Conference, which ended without agreement on 10 November 1910 and he too insisted on a second election. The King also agreed secretly that if the government won a majority he would create sufficient Liberal peers to override the Conservative veto.

> **Herbert Henry Asquith** (1852–1928) was Home Secretary in Gladstone's Cabinet of 1894, and replaced Campbell-Bannerman as Liberal Party leader and Prime Minister in 1908. His premiership saw Lloyd George's 'People's Budget', the clash with the House of Lords, and the outbreak of war in 1914. He formed a coalition government in 1915, but was ousted a year later by Lloyd George over his handling of the war. He had a reputation for drinking (hence his nickname 'Squiff'), and had a string of apparently platonic relationships with much younger women, writing to one, Venetia Stanley, during Cabinet meetings. (See *Asquith* by Stephen Bates, in this series.)

If the Conservatives won the December election the Lords' veto would be preserved but on what platform should the party stand? Opinion was divided whether or not tariff reform was an electoral boon or incubus. The December election was to be critical for Law's career. Senior Conservatives including the 'King of Lancashire', Lord Derby, hatched a plan that, if successful, would resolve the tariff reform controversy for good. This required a leading tariff reformer standing in a Lancashire free trade constituency. Sensing an opportunity, Law agreed to surrender Dulwich for the highly marginal North West Manchester. Vacating Dulwich for Manchester was a press stunt and a means of boosting Law to the highest levels of the party. Law's campaign generated huge national press coverage and the papers associated with Northcliffe, Garvin, Blumenfeld and Gwynne all gave prominence to his gallant 'sacrifice'. This was a 'win-win' situation for Law. He left Dulwich with a promise from Derby that if defeated in North West Manchester he would be quickly found a seat in Lancashire. Law enhanced his reputation as a good party man and, win or lose, he would increase his stature, earning the respect and gratitude of the party grandees. Law was defeated by 445 votes but his disappointment was tempered by the knowledge that he had received a major infusion of political capital. Derby shoehorned Law into the Bootle constituency where he doubled the Conservative majority in the March 1911 by-election. In June he was made a Privy Councillor.

The January and December elections produced no major change. The Conservatives drew with the Liberals in seats but Irish support meant the government's majority was as secure as ever. By the summer of 1911 it was inevitable that the Liberals would move against the veto. The Parliament Bill removed the Lords' power over all money bills and it was restricted to a suspensory veto on all other legislation for two successive parliamentary sessions. The bill also reduced the duration of a Parliament from seven to five years. Unaware of the King's pledge, many thought Asquith was bluffing, while others believed the King, as a good Tory, would never agree. When in June 1911 Asquith revealed George V's secret promise to create sufficient peers to force through constitutional reform the Conservatives were thrown into turmoil. Should they resist or surrender? Balfour opposed outright resistance. Law agreed, arguing there was a world of difference between the King creating enough peers to give the Liberals parity and creating sufficient to swamp the Conservative peers. Doing so would complete the transfer of legislative power to the executive and remove any hope of the party delaying obnoxious Liberal bills. If a large number of peers voted against the Parliament Bill before the creation of the Liberal peers, thereby rejecting the leadership's advice, Lansdowne, the leader in the Lords, and Balfour would resign. The party should accept the Parliament Bill because the alternative was worse. With a Liberal majority in the Lords the government would unleash a legislative firestorm of Home Rule, the disestablishment of the Welsh church and the manipulation of constituency boundaries.[30]

The 1911 Parliament Act passed on 11 August by 131 votes to 114. Its 'inner meaning' was as 'a charter by the aid of which Home Rule is to be the reward of the Nationalist faction, Disestablishment and Disendowment the prize of the Welsh faction, with "One Man One Vote", and, if time permits, other measures to sweeten the never-satisfied palate of the Radical-Socialist faction'.[31] The party was in a sour mood, with the various factions glowering at each other, frustrated by the years of opposition and its inability to deflect a government attacking fundamental Conservative interests. Balfour's hedging on the Parliament Act spawned the editor of the *National Review* Leo Maxse's 'BMG' (Balfour Must Go) campaign.[32] Tired and dispirited, Balfour resigned on 8 November 1911. This was hardly unexpected but, to the despair of the Chief Whip and Arthur Steel-Maitland, the party chairman, it was obvious the choice of a successor could split the party. The candidates, Austen Chamberlain (the tariff reformer) and Walter Long (representing the landed interest), had strong blocs of support which made them divisive. Even before Balfour resigned Law was being mentioned as a compromise candidate. The Chief Whip was initially dismissive; 'Bonar Law won't do. He seems almost to be retiring from politics so sporadic is his attendance ... he is more reserved and unapproachable every day.'[33] By early November Law's candidacy was viable because he was the 'least worst' option.

One way to avoid a split was for Chamberlain or Long to create an overwhelming majority and so avoid a vote. Neither could, so an alternative strategy was a compromise candidate. Law's candidacy meshed neatly with the party managers' desire to avoid a vote and keep Long out. Law could have lived with Chamberlain but not Long, who had the largest number of votes. Law's intention was to lay down a marker for the contest that would inevitably follow the election of either Chamberlain or Long. Two candidates pointed to a straight up and down vote; three implied two ballots in which the candidate with the least number of votes dropped out. Assuming Law would come third – he had about 40 votes – how would his votes be distributed? What price, if any, would Law demand for a recommendation? Long's supporters let it be known that if Long lost they would vote for Law to stop Chamberlain. Law's tactical goal was to promote deadlock and it is likely that he would have advised his supporters to vote for whichever candidate was winning. As a tariff reformer Law was more of a direct threat to Chamberlain and he came under pressure to withdraw, which only reinforced his determination. As a good party man Law was vulnerable to charges of ambition at the party's expense.

As late as 10 November it was widely believed Long was winning, Law could not win on a straight vote but his votes could hold the balance. Chamberlain and Long eventually agreed to withdraw in Law's favour but not for each other. Mutual withdrawal made Law's elevation certain. Law had doubts, 'his shortcomings were numerous – that as a widower and of humble means mean he could not entertain etc', which Balcarres clearly thought disingenuous.[34] Law was denigrated as the third-best man, inexperienced, lacking social status and linked to dubious characters; but he united the party. Many could not understand why Long and Chamberlain withdrew and 'there is now a greater feeling of discontent about than at any previous time, and many of the supporters of each protagonist think their man has been jockeyed out. I fear that Monday's meeting [the Carlton Club] may now be a stormy one.'[35]

Law's translation from 40 votes to anointed leader was remarkable. The 1911 contest 'brings out with stark clarity, the qualities which Conservatives seek in their leaders'. Chamberlain and Long could not win over the other's partisans. Law, however, would have lost against both so he needed to avoid a vote to become leader. So 'for the Conservatives, the best leader is not necessarily the person with majority support, but rather the one who can best hold the party together'.[36] Law ceased to be divisive. The Chief Whip sensed an overwhelming desire for unity and 'all doubts and hesitations had vanished'. Law judged his audience perfectly and his speech was greeted with applause; 'On breaking up many men consented to sink their differences and to work harmoniously under the new leader.'[37] Bridgeman wrote 'many beside myself have come to the conclusion that the adoption of B. Law is by far the best way out of the difficulty.' Law was elected unopposed. Bridgeman 'never thought so highly of our party ... Bonar Law was very nervous & very modest, but he made a good impression, & we all parted with the feeling that "we are all jolly good fellows" & so we really are.'[38]

Law had been positioning himself for a leadership run from 1908. Associated with the 1908 *Unauthorised Programme*, he remained lukewarm on whether or not social reform was profitable for Conservatives. On tariff reform Law avoided identification with extremes whilst making his scepticism about free trade clear. He remained loyal to the leadership, avoided dubious connections, playing a constructive role in finding solutions to the party's difficulties, and contested North West Manchester. Though a hedger on the Parliament Bill he was not out of step with the party and his and hostility to socialism and Home Rule were unimpeachable. His attacks on the Liberals made him a star performer. Law trod a delicate path but the impression left is of a politician positioning himself on the median Conservative MP. Though impossible to demonstrate, Law's actions have a logic pointing to a leadership challenge. He could not, of course, have predicted when, or if, Balfour would resign but when Balfour did resign was excellently placed as a compromise. How did the party react?

As late as 1916 some thought electing Law had been a serious error. Not 'a public school man', Law lacked depth: 'It's this d – d cleverness which always thinks the straightforward course too stupid to be right, which is undoing us, and the more you get so-called businessmen & pushers into politics the more you will have of it.'[39] At the instant Bridgeman was writing this 'the straightforward course' was

'Bonar Law was very nervous & very modest, but he made a good impression, & we all parted with the feeling that "we are all jolly good fellows" & so we really are.'

BRIDGEMAN

leading young public school officers and their men directly into German machine gun fire on the Somme on the orders of public school men. The perennial Conservative suspicion of 'being too clever by half' meant subtlety and strategic thinking were mistaken for lack of principle or, as a public school man might have had it, 'bottom'. The state of politics required more than 'nice-but-dim' and for policy to be based on more than a straight left to the jaw. Some grumbled about having a leader 'in trade' who was not only middle class, but from the Scottish and colonial middle class: 'Lady Londonderry is fulminating because B. Law isn't a country magnate.'[40] The Lady Bracknell tendency was in a minority. Whilst Law inspired loyalty from his MPs and the party, many found it difficult to weigh him up: 'The rank and file thought that he was a good man and was an excellent speaker but that he was not really one of them; he was the new type. Everybody liked him, even most of his opponents liked him – and they felt that he was only second-class.'[41] Those who thought Law second-class came to rue their underestimation. In the months immediately after his election Law tended to postpone decisions and not pronounce on issues that would cause trouble in the party. Nevertheless, 'all or nearly all look upon [Law] as an unqualified success … He has hit hard. He economises time, and spares words. Our men like this.' The political consequences were that, 'The confidence of the party has greatly risen during the last month. Men who distrusted BL have revised their views. They like his demeanour, and find him far more attractive as a speaker than was anticipated.'[42] Law's leadership style embraced a willingness to attack and a determination to keep his options open.

Law's sole motivation was unity achieved by aggressively confronting the Liberals and making peace with the big beasts in the Conservative jungle – Long, Chamberlain and Curzon

– and there was the possible problem of Balfour. In fact, none of these were to intrigue seriously against Law and whatever doubts or disagreements they entertained they kept them to themselves or articulated them in private. Law felt vulnerable because of his limitations on foreign, imperial and defence questions 'but he has time to learn, and I fancy will receive the help of very willing colleagues'.[43] The more senior Conservatives saw of Law, the more they liked and his confidence grew. Issues of party management prompted Law's caution; caution was often interpreted as indecision.

Law supported Central Office reforms designed to create a more effective campaigning party, improved fundraising (by 1914 the party had an income of over £600,000), and eventual merger with the Liberal Unionists. John Boraston and Malcom Fraser were appointed principal agent and the party's first press director respectively, to boost the party's effectiveness. Law cultivated good relations with the press and ensured the Conservative press remained in Conservative hands. The shadow cabinet, largely moribund and hitherto reliant on Balfour, was rejuvenated and despite tensions between members worked relatively well, although Law preferred to work on a bi-lateral basis with colleagues. Law was also determined to spend as much time as possible in the Smoking Room with his MPs. Given his prodigious consumption of tobacco this, unlike socialising with party bigwigs, was no hardship. By the end of the year there seemed 'a curious and almost dramatic change of atmosphere ... we are for the first time since 1906 attacking with the conviction of impending success'.[44] Law's problems, however, were about to begin.

Chapter 3: Tariff Reform

Law's position on this issue is invariably defined by Chamberlain's reporting of Law's confession that before 1914 he only really cared about tariff reform and Ulster. However, these concerns have to be viewed through the lens of Law's primordial political concern: party unity. Throughout his career tariff reform repeatedly split the party whereas Ulster united it. Both issues went to the heart of Conservatism but Ulster was a far more visceral issue. His speeches on Ulster, in contrast to the insipidity of those on tariff reform, were aggressive, indeed brutal, and consciously so. Ireland also demonstrated his flexibility. He evinced little reluctance to abandon the Southern Unionists: his main concern was Ulster. Law's object was always to maintain party unity; any issue that jeopardised electoral success would be dropped. For Law, then, caring about an issue was not the inevitable prelude to action.

Law's first major Commons speech was on the Hicks-Beach duties on imported corn. Imposed as a revenue raising measure during the South African War, repeal was interpreted by many as a manifestation of the simmering free trade – protection row in the party. Law criticised those *with whom the principles of Free Trade have assumed the sanctity of a religion, and has happens with all religions there has grown up around Free Trade a bundle of superstitions not less tenaciously held than the central doctrines themselves.* Law felt the same about ardent tariff reformers. Drawing on his business experience, Law recalled that when competition from US pig iron developed, one of the unions, hitherto a supporter of free trade approached the iron masters with a proposal for a boycott. Protection, Law concluded, need not be imposed because *it will come from the working man when he sees his employment disappearing and the articles he himself makes made in other countries and sold at his own door at a lower price.* Law's tariff reform was, in fact, the protection of manufacturing. The industrial cities wanted cheap food and so would vote against food taxes. Law believed the laws of supply and demand would keep food prices low and the importer in effect paid any tax. Law urged free traders keep an open mind: *They imagine they are going to raise the country to the old agitation. They are going, perhaps, to send out pictures of the big loaf and little loaf. If that is their idea, I would say to them that they are like what was said of the Stuarts: they have learned nothing and forgotten nothing.*[1] The world had changed so much since 1846 and the challenge from foreign industry was manifest. Politicians would be better employed protecting domestic industry and prosperity, Law concluded.

This was not the speech of a partisan. It was a moderate, pragmatic, rational argument for piecemeal protection based on the premise that what had been desirable in the 19th century when Britain's industrial pre-eminence was unchallenged was not so now. Competition from Germany and the United States, whose domestic markets were protected by tariffs, justified a case-by-case review and if necessary, retaliation. Law's business experience enabled him to become one of the party's economics experts and this led directly to his appointment as Parliamentary Secretary to the Board of Trade in the re-shuffle when Balfour became Prime Minister in July 1902.

Law had taken his first step on the ministerial ladder but his duties were neither remarkable nor onerous. He dealt with, for example, shipping statistics, trade statistics and lighthouses, not high policy. A speech on the Sugar Convention sheds light on Law's conception of tariff reform. Citing the success of the German sugar beet industry, Law pointed out that it had grown behind a protective barrier. The local economy had flourished and prosperity increased, a practical demonstration of the value of tariffs. American iron producers manufactured two or three times as much iron as their British competitors. Not only were their unit costs lower, they enjoyed substantial market power. American industry, protected by a tariff, was *in the hands of a few people, who are quite ready to use their power to crush competition.* US iron makers would exploit Britain's open markets to wipe out the British industry. The result would be unemployment and social unrest: *If such a thing were to happen, the men connected with the iron industry and their fellow working-men throughout the country would give this House a lesson in the elementary principles of political economy which we would not easily forget.*[2] Parliament *could not allow a vital industry to be destroyed* and this principle operated with greater force where nascent domestic industries and those of the Empire were concerned. Britain had to defend itself. International agreements like the Sugar Convention would help British industry by reducing subsidies and the possibility of retaliation would encourage competitors to behave reasonably.

Law denied any connection between Britain's 19th-century commercial and industrial pre-eminence and free trade because the country's supremacy was greatest before 1846. Cheapness should not be the be-all-and-end-all of trade and fiscal policy whose aim should be *free exchange at natural prices.*[3] Low prices indicated monopoly power, which resulted in poor working and living conditions and, hence, social discontent. Retaliation or protection would not produce permanently high prices because of the laws of supply and demand, so retaliation and protection helped markets work. Extreme free trade or protection produced too much government involvement in industry's affairs and so distorted the market.

In 1909, in a debate on fiscal retaliation, Law complained about a lack of clarity on what its advocates meant by free trade and identified a fundamental flaw: the conflict between the general and the specific interest. *One hon. Gentleman*, Law told the House, *a friend of mine, who is a member for Kent, is willing to live or die for Free Trade, but hops are produced in Kent. Hops are different. A duty on hops would be an unmixed advantage to the people of the country.* This contradiction would eventually lead to free trade's collapse as the collective interest was merely an aggregation of the specific, and the latter would overcome the former. Advocates of protective tariffs had recognised where their interest lay in a changing world.[4]

Though a tariff reformer, Law was neither a zealot nor true believer: 'when Bonar Law was first appointed Joe had said, "He is not a Tariff Reformer"', and, Amery concluded, 'there is a real element of truth in that'.[5] For Law tariff reform was a tactic not a strategy, a weapon to promote fair trade with each case considered on its merits. Law was sceptical about the political feasibility of Chamberlain's project and as an ex-member of the Glasgow iron-ring he was acutely conscious of the complex dynamics of trade and the fragility of business confidence. When Joe Chamberlain died, Law's encomium hinted his attitude to Chamberlain and tariff reform had shifted. *At the time when I first entered this House*, Law declared, *I was still young enough, and, indeed, hope I still am, to be a hero worshipper, and for me at that time, the essence of my political faith was belief in Mr Chamberlain.*[6] Law retained his admiration of the man but was never committed to Chamberlain's vision of a grand imperial project and Law's scepticism increased as tariff reform shattered the party. Law used the Board of Trade to build his reputation and credibility as a good party man who regarded unity as the *sine qua non* of effective politics.

Law had little time for those who, married to doctrinal purity, encouraged electoral failure. After 1906 the divided and decimated Conservative Party was split between three factions. First, a disparate group of free traders/free fooders, Cecilian Conservatives and Liberal Unionists hostile to tariff reform (31 MPs); Chamberlainite 'whole hoggers' who became increasingly inflexible and doctrinaire (79 MPs); and 'a mass of fence-sitters and moderates' grouped around Balfour. Some were free traders; some tariff reformers of various hues but all were united by a fear of the political consequences of an unelectable Conservative Party.[7] On the Opposition front bench Law was one of only five 'Chamberlainites' but most of the 'coming men' were identified as tariff reformers. Coming from manufacturing and commercial backgrounds their influence was rising and Law was seen as the archetype.

At the time when I first entered this House, I was still young enough, and, indeed, hope I still am, to be a hero worshipper, and for me at that time, the essence of my political faith was belief in Mr Chamberlain.

BONAR LAW

The main obstacle to the tariff reformers was the Balfourite compromisers. Central to this group was the landed interest, which though not ideologically hostile to tariff reform, feared the loss of the agricultural vote, as Chamberlain's intention was to protect colonial not British farmers. They tended to be socially dismissive of 'Birmingham', or in Law's case, 'Glasgow'. Tariffs reflected a deeper divide in the party between the cautious defenders of the *status quo* and the proponents of radical reform. Free fooders tended to favour the former whereas Chamberlainites were associated with a more 'progressive' Conservatism, but neither was representative of the party. For Whole Hoggers the party was an instrument to realise a vision and, if necessary, be abandoned; others, including Law, saw the party as a core political institution whose vitality was an essential to constitutional equilibrium. The party would be fatally damaged by an insistence on doctrinal purity, leaving government in Radical hands.

The tariff reform ascendancy encouraged rumours of plots to purge the party, a purge in which Law has been implicated. This was the largely mythical 'Confederacy', led by Sir Henry Page Croft.[8] Law was in contact with members of the 'Confederacy' trying to engineer a compromise. From the 'Confederacy's' perspective Law was a sympathiser who was rising up the party and with whom it was wise to maintain friendly relations. Given Law's political ethic and commitment to unity, involvement with a secret society made no sense. The Unionist free traders' problems were not caused by secret society conspiracies but were the consequence of a party polarising after a disastrous election, a party divided on its response to Lloyd George's budget and the Lords' veto, and the battle within the constituency associations over tariff reform. In March 1909 the Chief Whip, bemoaning backbench apathy and inactivity and the dearth of talent on the front bench, described Law as essential.[9] It was at this point that the bottom fell out of Law's world with his wife's death on 31 October. Tempted to withdraw from public life, Law was tempted back by his colleagues and politics soon absorbed him.

Law worked hard to revitalise the party's appeal. Sceptical about programmatic politics, Law's defeat by Barnes and Lloyd George's budget forced him to consider the direction of politics. Labour's emergence, the threat to 'sound finance',

Lloyd George's predilection for direct taxation were frontal attacks on tariff reform. Radicalism promised that 'property', especially landed aristocratic property, would pay for old age pensions and battleships. Lloyd George embraced confiscatory taxation and class antagonism. It heralded the end of the free trade political project and was the harbinger of socialism. The combination of mass democracy and free trade would force its advocates to adopt confiscatory taxation whereas taxing foreign capital was indirect, fairer and capable of providing all the resources government required.[10] Governments justifying legislation by the 'popular will' would redistribute wealth, offering voters something for nothing. In this new politics principles of sound finance were replaced by electoral bribery for party advantage.[11]

It is our aim, as it was the aim of Disraeli throughout his long life, to be the party not of a class, but the party of the nation.

BONAR LAW

In his first speech as Party Leader Law presented tariff reform as a positive alternative to Lloyd George-ism. *It is,* Law told conference, *our aim, as it was the aim of Disraeli throughout his long life* – (cheers) – *to be the party not of a class, but the party of the nation.* Growing demands for redistribution had been fomented by Lloyd George's budget. High direct taxation and free trade had caused capital flight and the loss of British jobs to foreign competition, encouraging the upsurge in industrial unrest and a decline in working class living standards. Fiscal reform would reduce unemployment, reduced business costs (including taxation) thereby boosting working class living standards. Law cited Germany's policy approvingly: *We must do the same.*[12]

LG's 'People's Budget' was confiscatory and motivated by class hatred, expressing the change in the nature of politics as a result of the 1906 election. Having been defeated by a socialist, Law felt this change keenly. On 4 November 1909 the budget passed the Commons and was then defeated in the Lords. An election was called for 15 January 1910 and the Liberal government announced its intention of reforming the Lords' veto power. In an era when 'democracy' appeared to be morphing into 'socialism' before their eyes, Conservatives like Law saw the party not merely as a political or electoral contrivance but as part of a delicate system of checks and balances, as part of the constitution. The Liberal assault on the constitution was part of an attempt to destroy the party which represented one of the main bastions against radicalism and socialism. The January election represents the high point of whole-hogger influence. Seventy-four per cent of candidates considered Chamberlain's programme the chief issue but the results were mixed. The Conservatives recovered ground lost in 1906 with 273 seats to the Liberals 275, down from 401, but the Liberals could rely on Redmond's 82 Irish Nationalist MPs and 40 Labour MPs, an impregnable majority of 124. This was a profoundly destabilising outcome. Chamberlain's programme had failed; there was no Conservative government to defend the *status quo*. Pragmatic tariff reformers were deeply disenchanted because it failed where it was supposed to win, in the industrial North. Critics focussed on food taxes as responsible for working class rejection of the party and this encouraged a realignment of factions in the party.

In December the Liberals won 272 seats (-1) and the Conservatives 276 (-3); Labour had 42 (+2) and the Irish Nationalists 84 (+2). The election therefore resolved nothing. The Liberal victory meant the Lords had no grounds to refuse to pass the budget. Their use of the veto against convention and precedent meant the Liberals would seek to guarantee their programme, including Home Rule, by eradicating the veto. The Lords' veto was seen by many Conservatives as the last line of defence against radicalism: abolition of the veto was a premonition of an apocalypse culminating in the end of Empire and socialism. The overriding Conservative object was to resist the threat to the established order and resistance, it was believed, would pull the party together. The party could be forgiven for thinking that the January election demonstrated the pendulum was swinging away from the Liberals despite the Conservative commitment to duties on imported food. Balfour was of the view that, on balance, food taxes were hindering the pendulum. Law agreed, as we have seen, to campaign on tariff reform in Manchester. This campaign had wide political implications. Law agreed with Derby that the food taxes should be toned down. Derby also suggested to Law that if elected the party should hold a referendum on food taxes. Law was convinced but did not commit himself until Balfour did so in his Albert Hall speech in November. The 1910 elections convinced Law that tariff reform and food taxes were dangerous for the party at a time when it was, perhaps, the last, obstacle to radicalism running riot. The party's mood had shifted: 'it is consequently quixotic to expect that the old amicable relations between politicians in private life can continue on their former footing.'[13]

Law's position was influenced by Ireland's re-emergence from the political deep-freeze. The Parliament Act gave the Conservatives an ability to delay controversial legislation and the most controversial would, given the government's dependence on the Irish Nationalists, be Home Rule. They could not, however, stop its passage. Ulster members and Southern Loyalists feared that saw the party's stance on Lords reform presaged a capitulation on Home Rule. However, the party could unite around opposing Home Rule but first it had to find a solution to food taxes. This became Law's task.

Subsequently, the Chief Whip complained ruefully about

'the thraldom of the food taxes' that had been 'imposed on us by the machine (or as others say "by Birmingham")'. Food taxes were 'a crippling burden', and Unionist MPs 'say that they are amazed that we should have tolerated them for so long, and the machine should have so successfully maintained the imposture of their popularity and demand. There is much truth in this.'[14] Balfour had committed a Unionist government to a referendum on food taxes on condition that a Liberal government held a referendum on Home Rule. This last-minute attempt, supported by Law, to persuade free trade-inclined floating voters to vote Unionist failed. Home Rule was not put to a referendum, so the Conservative referendum pledge was neutralised but the pledge triggered the first major crisis of Law's leadership.

There were two broad attitudes to tariff reform after Balfour's resignation. The first regarded it and especially food taxes as responsible for electoral defeat. They were a distraction from the fight against Home Rule and damaged Unionist support. The second regarded tariff reform as essential for national and imperial interests. Food taxes were an alternative source of revenue and gave preference to imperial produce. Law was closest to the latter position and not especially concerned by Balfour's pledge, which he regarded as a tactical-electoral manoeuvre. Law was eventually compelled to come to a position on the referendum. *The position is, as you know*, Law wrote to Lord Selbourne, *very difficult, and how it will develop I do not know. What I am sure of is that while the great bulk of our Members are agreed in desiring, to get rid of the food duties, none of them have any idea as to what the policy of the Party would then be.*[15]

Law recognised that food taxes damaged the party with agricultural and industrial voters, diverted attention away from tariff reform's positive aspects and from the struggle over Home Rule. Most importantly, they threatened to split the party. His personal inclination was to do nothing but mounting disquiet led him to conclude action could not be postponed. The Shadow Cabinet of 29 February 1912 concluded the party would have to keep food taxes but the referendum pledge would be dropped. This policy would not be made public. As early as February Law was contemplating his resignation as a solution to the problem. In August 1912 the Shadow Cabinet agreed to repudiate the referendum. Law disliked these meetings because they often degenerated into a row between Chamberlain and Long, which further reinforced his belief that party unity required postponing a decision. Any internal crisis would reduce the impact of the party's attacks on the Liberal government. This proved unsustainable and on 14 November Lord Lansdowne, the party's leader in the Lords, delivered a speech at the annual Unionist conference at the Albert Hall. Lansdowne announced that as the Liberals had refused a referendum on Home Rule, the Conservatives held they were released from Balfour's referendum pledge. Lansdowne's speech appeared to go down well and Law's slashing attack on the government was greeted with rapture by the conference.

Lansdowne achieved the opposite, initiating a rebellion in Lancashire. Alderman Archibald Salvidge, the boss of Liverpool, and Lord Derby, the leader of Lancashire Conservatism, announced Lancashire would hold a county conference on 21 December to debate the new policy. Initially sanguine, Law soon became alarmed and seriously contemplated reinstating the pledge to placate Lancashire. Calling a second full party meeting with no guarantee of success, however, could only do this. Law had no doctrinal objection to abandoning food taxes but 'he should not do so in response to active and open pressure.' The consequences appeared dire: 'Candidates ready to retire, Press more and more hostile, Birmingham itself vacillating – cost of living making food taxes more and more hated: nine out of ten of our MPs anxious for an exit from our difficulty.'[16] Law (and Lansdowne's) resignations became a distinct possibility.

Law attempted to 'clarify' the party's position in a speech in Aitken's strategically important Ashton-under-Lyne constituency on 16 December. The Ashton speech sought to by-pass the crisis by making food taxes dependent on an imperial conference to establish a system of preference and food taxes would not operate until after a second election. Law was vulnerable on two grounds: Aitken had packed the meeting so the speech's enthusiastic reception was deceptive because it infuriated whole hoggers and tariff reformers. Both *The Times* and the *Daily Mail* were hostile and neither Derby nor Salvidge were mollified. Far from resolving the crisis, the speech stoked the fires and Law resolved to resign if the policy was rejected by the Lancashire conference. To avoid this Derby persuaded the Lancashire Conservatives to postpone the conference for three weeks. The meeting could only be interpreted as a direct challenge to Law, who resented it, but it was articulating a real and dangerous problem. By Christmas 1912 the party and Law's leadership was in serious crisis.

Law had come to the view that resignation might be part of the solution. However, resignation might be a weapon not a weakness. Over Christmas Law and Lansdowne decided to attack by resigning at a special party meeting and the result, as they intended, was consternation. Only some 40 MPs opposed Law's policy and the bulk of the party would be glad to see the back of the commitment. Moreover, 'The sentiment of affection and regard for B.L. continues undiminished. He can readily secure a unanimous vote of confidence, but acquiescence in our present policy, no! The vast bulk of our MPs and candidates heartily desire a change.'[17]

On 6 January Edward Carson, the Ulster Unionist leader, learned to his horror that the referendum pledge and food taxes (about which he cared little) might lead to Law's resignation, seriously damaging the party's fight against Home Rule (about which Carson cared a great deal). Carson used Goulding to organise a petition amongst MPs urging Law and Lansdowne not to resign. Law was well aware what was going on. Law made it clear that he would only accept such a plea if it were signed by a large majority of MPs. To do otherwise, Law believed, would convey an impression of inconsistency and weakness, so undermining his legitimacy and authority. The result was the January Memorial. Much was riding on it: 'A real crisis — for we are not only in danger of losing our leaders, but equally of losing the Union, the Welsh Church, and Tariff Reform into the bargain.'[18] Excluding frontbenchers, the Speaker, those Conservatives who were ill, abroad or absent, 231 MPs signed it, with only six MPs refusing.

Born in 1854, Edward Carson was a lawyer who became counsel to the attorney general for Ireland in 1887 when Balfour was Secretary of State, and was involved in the prosecution of Irish nationalists. One of the outstanding advocates of his generation, he was also a staunch Unionist and became leader of the Irish Unionists in 1910. After the near-outbreak of civil war in Ireland was put off by the First World War, he was Attorney General in Asquith's coalition, then First Lord of the Admiralty under Lloyd George. Raised to the peerage in 1921 as Baron Carson of Duncairn, he died in 1935

Amery disparaged MPs who, thrown into a panic by the resignation threat, urged a 'blind following of Bonar Law whatever he did'. However, Amery recognised the strength of the feeling in the party, hence 'a tremendous effort was made to induce him to stay on at all costs'.[19] Bridgeman could not understand why Law was taking so hard a line. He saw nothing wrong or discreditable 'in bowing to the general wishes of a large majority of your supporters' and Law's resignation 'would be disastrous to the party'. Over Christmas and the New Year the reason for Law's intransigence became clear. Bridgeman noted that 'it became evident that there was a huge majority who thought the "food taxes" must go for the time being at least, and a unanimous wish of a very intense character that Bonar Law should not resign'.[20] On 13 January Law graciously accepted the Memorial. The compromise was that a Unionist government, if it found food duties to be necessary and acceptable to both the UK and Dominion parliaments, would not implement them until after a second election. The result was universal relief in the party. Law pronounced the matter closed but made it clear that he now expected the party, united under his leadership, to vigorously attack the government.

The referendum crisis is fundamental to understanding Law as a politician. Teetering on the edge of defeat Law counter-attacked, routed his opponents and entrenched his authority as leader. The party leader's tasks are, Bogdanor argues, 'first, he must display competence and efficiency at his task; secondly, he must be perceived as an electoral asset, and have a reasonable prospect of carrying the country in a general election; thirdly, he must retain the allegiance of the Conservative backbenchers; and fourthly, he must retain the support of the party in the country. Above all, a Conservative leader must not split the party.'[21]

By late 1912 and early 1913 Law had achieved three of these four and he was to use the Ulster crisis to map out an electoral strategy. The crisis developed from a misjudgement by Law but the outcome was entirely in his favour and he drew three lessons from the crisis. First, it ran out of control because of poor intelligence about the party's reaction to Lansdowne's speech; second, food taxes damaged the party; and third, unity and discipline were fragile commodities. 'Back-me-or-sack-me' ploys are frequently suicidal but Law gambled and keeping his nerve definitively demonstrated his authority and indispensability.

In effect Law dictated the Memorial's content, strengthening himself immeasurably by determining the conditions under which he would consent to continue to lead the party and then compelling MPs to accept these terms under the threat of his resignation, despite having (apparently) made concessions. Law used the crisis and the Memorial to ram home to the Unionist party that there was no alternative to his leadership, thus transforming his leadership and himself as a politician. Law also developed a strategy, which he used on several subsequent occasions to resolve internal crises to his advantage. First, when faced by serious unrest Law would transform the issue into a matter of resignation. He presented the party with a binary choice ('back me or sack me') leaving no space, as in 1911, for a compromise candidate. Second, Law acted ruthlessly to maximise the centre ground and isolate his opponents; and thirdly, Law used crises to revivify and bolster his authority by forcing the party to come to him in a *de facto* vote of confidence. The referendum crisis revealed Law was capable of political creativity of a very high order indeed. This made him extremely dangerous.

How committed ideologically was Law to tariff reform? Law's contemporaries, as well as Law himself, noted his identification with Chamberlain and Law was clearly a protectionist. In 1908–09 a common jibe in the Commons was that all Law's speeches, irrespective of topic, were about tariff reform.

Law's tariff reform was, however, pragmatic. Tariff reform embraced a multiplicity of positions up to and including the creation of an Imperial *zollverein*. As a programme of imperial integration and domestic political realignment it was infinitely more radical than protecting industry from foreign competition. The free trade–tariff reform cleavage transformed it into an issue of party management and electability. This transformation was of enormous significance for Law's politics.

On 26 January 1912 at the Albert Hall Law confessed that *For eight years I have advocated this policy ... But I am not blind.* Law believed Unionists could not, and should not, abandon tariff reform as this was the best policy for the country and Empire but tariff reform aroused fierce passions. Once unleashed these could shatter the party and *by shattering that party we should destroy the only bulwark against the present Government*. The choice facing Unionist free traders was *between Tariff Reform, which they dislike, and Lloyd Georgeism, which they detest*; the latter could unite the whole party. He concluded, *we are Tariff Reformers, but we are also Conservatives; and we shall take care that any change in our fiscal system for which we are responsible is as little revolutionary as possible.*[22] Chamberlain was correct. Law was 'not one of us', because tariff reform was a tactic not a strategy, a tool of economic management not a grand imperial project, but Law *was* a tariff reformer. There is, however, commitment and commitment. Law's 'commitment' must to be viewed through the lenses of electoral defeat and the Liberal government's legislation. Law could perceive no virtue in any policy that manifestly prevented the party from winning elections. The answer to the question 'was Law committed ideologically to tariff reform?' is, not much.

Law's foremost concern was, and remained, party unity. He was determined to avoid any course of action that might so damage the party that Liberals, Radicals, Socialists and the Irish were left in possession of the country's political institutions. The party was more than a political tool; it was an integral part of the constitution. Law's logic was simple: a divided Unionist party would not win elections, if it did not win elections Unionism could not form a government and the only alternative to a Unionist government were increasingly radical Liberal governments. By 1912 the most serious threat was Home Rule and Law knew that all Conservatives would unite around the defence of the Union. Preserving the Union was more important than tariff reform.

Chapter 4: Ulster

For most of Law's career Ireland dominated both Conservative politics and British politics in general. Law's personal connection with Ulster, where his father had been born and where he died and where his elder brother practised medicine, does not explain his position. Nor does religion. Law was, as we have seen, uninterested in religion. He found Ulster Protestantism's anti-Catholic bigotry distasteful, although his rhetoric reinforced that bigotry, and he employed a Catholic nanny for his children. Law's stance was based, first, on what he perceived as an unbridgeable political gulf between the Protestant North and Catholic South over Ireland's relationship with the imperial metropol: antagonistic majorities appealing to their democratic rights, demanding the irreconcilable.

Law's apparent willingness to provoke civil war has puzzled and outraged. How can we explain a Conservative leader endorsing armed resistance to an elected government, putting the Crown under enormous pressure to revive (at best) moribund powers, and fomenting mutiny in the Army? All of these were expressed in some of the most incendiary language ever heard from a parliamentarian. Rejecting explanations such as inexperience, hysteria, and bigotry, or that Law had lost his grip on reality, forces us back onto seeking a rational motive. What was Law's objective? He wanted a Conservative government. By-elections were moving in the

Conservatives' favour and the removal of the food tax incubus helped but the parliamentary arithmetic gave Law only one weapon: rhetoric. The aim was to force Asquith to call an election by convincing him that his Home Rule policy would result in disaster for himself, his party, and the country.

Law's, and the party's, strategy derived from A V Dicey's, *The Law and the Constitution* (1885) and *England's Case Against Home Rule* (1886). Dicey argued the constitution was grounded on absolute parliamentary sovereignty and the rule of law. However, a sovereign parliament could not be constrained by law because it could change the law by a simple majority vote. Absolute parliamentary sovereignty had, prior to Gladstone's conversion to Home Rule and the rise of mass democracy, been constrained by convention, the House of Lords veto, the Monarchy, and an inter- and intra-elite consensus on what constituted 'good' governance. By 1912 only the Monarchy remained. Dicey, a committed Unionist, argued Home Rule was so fundamental a constitutional change it could not be implemented other than by a 'special' process. Unfortunately the doctrine of parliamentary sovereignty meant there was no legal or procedural difference between 'ordinary' and 'constitutional' legislation. Confronted by a government which justified Home Rule by its majority, but which refused to hold an election or referendum, then civil disobedience and rebellion became legitimate methods of resistance. The removal of the Lords' veto meant that Home Rule would become law under the 1911 Act in 1914 and the coherence of the Liberal majority meant Asquith had no need to dissolve until 1915, after the delay. The Liberals would then campaign on a radical manifesto based on land taxes and an extension of social welfare. Asquith had no incentive in the current structure of politics to call an election; Law wanted an election, which meant he had to

Ulster and the Presbyterians

Andrew Bonar Law once told Austen Chamberlain that the only two issues he cared intensely about were *Tariff reform and Ulster; all the rest was only part of the game.* And it was Ulster, which became the most hotly contested political issue in the three years leading up to the outbreak of the First World War. Bonar Law's feelings towards the Protestants of Northern Ireland can only be described as 'tribal' – harking back more than 300 years to the time when the link between Presbyterians and Northern Ireland came about as a result of the one of the most dangerous rebellions against Elizabeth I. Hugh O'Neill, the Catholic Earls of Tyrone and Tyrconnel, rose against, but were eventually defeated and fled into exile in France. On the lands forfeited by the fugitive Earls, colonies were planted – exclusively English and Scottish settlers, forbidden for the most part even to take Irish tenants.

While this official plantation was taking root in the western part of Ulster, another, unofficial influx of settlers was taking place in the eastern part of the province near Belfast. The eastern immigrants were Presbyterian Scots, dissenters from the Established Protestant church. The two settlements spread out to meet each other, but the demographic map of Northern Ireland reveals to this day the traces of the two original groupings. (Anthony Kenny, *The Road to Hillsborough* (Pergamon Press, London: 1986) pp 2ff.) It is to Ulster that Andrew Bonar Law's father moved back, when he retired as the Presbyterian minister of a small, mainly Scottish immigrant flock in New Brunswick, Canada. Although his son Andrew had been born in Canada and had never lived in his father's native Ulster, he visited him frequently there. He identified completely with the Ulster cause, and went well beyond the constitutional duty of a Leader of the Opposition in encouraging armed resistance by the Ulster Volunteer Force. In July 1913, he sent a message to an Orange demonstration saying: *Whatever steps they might feel compelled to take, whether they were constitutional, or whether in the long run they were unconstitutional, they had the whole of the Unionist Party under his leadership behind them.*

change the structure of politics in his favour. Hence, Law's rhetoric. The second aspect of Law's strategy was to persuade the King to intervene and, effectively, dismiss Asquith. Dicey thought this was going too far.

The government, Law maintained, had no mandate for such a momentous constitutional change and *they have done it at the bidding of a small faction in this House, whose votes they now depend upon ... they have made themselves their tools in abolishing a Constitution which is nothing to them.*[1] The result was the tyranny of the Southern Nationalist majority over the Unionist minority. Only an election in which a majority either endorsed or rejected the government's proposals could resolve this clash: *if the people of this country decide that they will make the experiment of Home Rule ... I should say I believe in representative government, and, however much you dislike it, you cannot compel the United Kingdom to keep up the present arrangement against their will, and I should say to the loyalists of Ireland, 'You have got to submit'.* However, Law continued, *if this or any other Government try to force through a measure on which there is good reason to believe the people of this country are not agreed, and to which those of us who abhor the Bill believe the people of this country are opposed, I would never, if I were one of those Irish loyalists, consent to have such a system forced upon me as part of a corrupt Parliamentary bargain.*

Law's gravest charge was that the Liberals were destroying representative government, which *rests on a convention and nothing more. It rests on the convention that a majority at any given time represents the balance of forces in the country. But majorities are not always stronger than minorities, and that convention can only continue to be respected so long as the majority uses its powers with moderation* – (hear, hear) – *and with a due regard to the convictions and the strength of those to whom thy are opposed.* (Hear, hear). *It cannot continue if the majority – and a small majority*

– tries to ride rough-shod over the minority. (Hear, hear).[2] For the minority Home Rule was a mortal threat that jeopardised their political and religious liberties and which threatened their identity as a people.

At the centre of Law's critique of Liberal governance and the Ulster question was the majority/minority relationship in representative government. The Prime Minister, Law charged, took it as axiomatic *that the House of Commons, returned by the electors of this country, represented those electors and was entitled to carry out its programme because the electors sent the Members here.*[3] This excluded minority opinion, the Opposition, the House of Lords and the Monarchy. For Law and many Conservatives this doctrine was literally revolutionary because it replaced the balanced constitution with the tyranny of the majority. This degree of subversion meant that the Conservatives could have only one object: *to get rid of the present Government* – (hear, hear and laughter) – *which from the beginning has been a danger to our country* – (hear, hear) – *and which is now tearing down the destructive path with ever increasing rapidity.*[4]

Ministers ignored the fact that *all experience and history show that there is an equal danger in putting too great a power into the hands of the House which exists by the votes of the electors.*[5] Any government wishing to introduce radical change needed an unequivocal parliamentary majority: *suppose a Budget such as that of 1909, which the authors of it admitted contained new principles, and suppose that after the fights … that Government had come back with a majority and had carried that Budget by a majority of one in this House. Does any reasonable man say that under those conditions such a Budget ought to become the law of the land in the country?*[6] This supposition carried even more force when the Constitution had been disturbed. The only solution was *an appeal to the people of this country, who are masters of the House of Lords and masters of His Majesty's Government.*[7]

The flaw in Law's argument was his assumption that a general election result would be definitive. If a government claiming to represent the majority refused to abide by constitutional convention and respect minority rights, as represented by the Opposition, it subverted the Constitution and encouraged division. The Opposition had a duty to resist by any means left open to it by the government. The sole constitutional means of resolving a majority-minority conflict was a general election. Combined, these produced a very high-risk strategy. What if the election did not produce the result the minority wanted? What if the result was equivocal? What if there was a decisive result but the minority refused to accept it? The rhetoric needed to force a government with a majority into calling a premature election might worsen the crisis. Faced by an onslaught, the government might choose to dig in and resist, whilst the Opposition might find itself fomenting civil unrest for party-political and anti-democratic purposes.

The 1912 Session, Law's first full one as leader, was dominated by Home Rule. Law's reply to the King's Speech was designed to put maximum pressure on Asquith. *[T]he Government*, Law asserted, *are trying, under the mask of constitutional government and methods, to exercise arbitrary and despotic power.* Home Rule could not be passed in conformity with commonly accepted norms of parliamentary government. If *he* [Asquith] *really attempts to carry out that programme ... I am absolutely certain that he will shatter to their foundations the Parliamentary institutions of this country.*[8] The new element was that the government had broken the 'social contract', shattering the norms of constitutional politics. If so, and if, as Law contended, the constitution was in abeyance then those subject to despotic power and the denial of constitutional rights could legitimately resort to other methods in defence of their rights. At Bootle on 7 December Law predicted Home Rule (*an utterly intolerable curse*) *would bring to Ireland and England, not peace, but a sword.* He warned, *there will be no shrinking from strong action. There will be no shrinking from any action which we think necessary to defeat one of the most ignoble conspiracies which has ever been formed against the liberties of free-born men.*[9] At the Albert Hall on 27 January 1912 Law emphasised the legitimacy of popular resistance to despotic power.

If they seriously attempt to carry out their programme when at least half the nation is against them, it will not be a representative government – it will not be a government at all; it will be the tyranny of a revolutionary Committee. If they make the attempt they will impose a strain upon our Parliamentary institutions which I am sure these institutions cannot bear.[10]

On Easter Sunday (9 April) Law spoke at the famous (or infamous) Unionist rally at the Royal Agricultural Society grounds in Belfast. Held under the largest Union Jack ever manufactured, a crowd of 100,000 heard Law declare: *There is no instance in history where force has been used by any nation to drive out their fellow-citizens. Great nations, great democratic nations, have indeed taken up arms to prevent their fellow-subjects from seceding. Is it conceivable that the British people would use force compel you to secede? Under any circumstances, your resistance would, I think, be irresistible.*[11]

Law returned to these themes in the House of Commons on 16 April when, as Leader of the Opposition, he responded to the introduction of the bill on 11 April. The bill's rationale, he contended, was that the Irish MPs, Asquith's majority, wanted it. Sovereignty would be fragmented and *It cannot, in the nature of things last*, because *Irishmen must either regard themselves as citizens of the United Kingdom, they must take their chance with the rest of us in the British House of Commons, in which they are representatives as much as we are* – [Hon. Members: 'More'.] – *... or they must be regarded as a separate nation ... entitled to all the rights of a nationality ...*[12]

If Law was correct and the bill could not be a final settlement, the logical end was independence for Ireland, which would trigger the Empire's break-up. Nationalist opinion would remain dissatisfied and, despite a reduction in their numbers at Westminster, would be a constant source of turbulence and turmoil. A Dublin parliament, on the other hand, would infuriate Ulster, which would never be reconciled. Home Rule would not take Ireland out of politics. Every contentious issue between the majority and minority would come to Westminster; Welsh, English and Scots MPs would resent Irish involvement in their affairs and the Nationalists might hold the balance of power. *Nothing is more certain*, Law concluded, *in this world than that one democratic Parliament cannot control another democratic Parliament.* Law confessed he was reluctant to speak on the religious aspects of Home Rule but strongly-held religious convictions would inevitably dominate Irish politics: *The Protestants of Ireland, nine-tenths of them at least, do believe that under this Parliament they will suffer disabilities.* Law hoped they were wrong but given the passions involved, *do not be under any illusion. The only safeguard is the tolerance of the Irish majority. There is no other.*

One million loyal subjects could not be dismissed as a small minority. Law compared the government's proposal to the Partition of Poland. *What*, he asked, *is regarded as one of the greatest crimes of despotism in the past? It is, and has always been considered, the transference of allegiance against their will of small nationalities.* The April gathering in Belfast was not just another protest meeting but something profound; *It represented the expression of the soul of a people – as I believe, a great people. They say they will not submit except by force to such a Government. How are you going to prevent that?* Law knew the risk he was taking but believed he had a wider duty. This was *to impress upon this House ... and to impress upon the country ... the reality of the situation ... These people in Ulster are under no illusion. They know they cannot fight the British Army* [A Hon. Member: 'They will try'] ... Law painted a stark picture: *The people of Ulster know that if the soldiers receive orders to shoot, it will be their duty to obey. They will have no ill-will against them for obeying. But ... these men believe, and are ready, in what they believe to be the cause of justice and liberty, to lay down their lives.*

Civilian deaths would be the personal responsibility of the Prime Minister because he would have given the order *to shoot down men whose only crime is that they refused to be driven out of our community and deprived of the privilege of British citizenship.* Loyalists, Law concluded, been forced to this extremity by a despotic government in thrall to a minority of MPs for whose support Asquith was prepared to betray the Constitution. Consequently, *We can imagine nothing which the Unionists in Ireland can do which will not be justified, against a trick of this kind. And you will not succeed. You have taught us to divide the United Kingdom ... you will not carry this Bill without submitting to the people of this country, and, if you make an attempt, you will succeed only in breaking our Parliamentary machine.* Incendiary rhetoric indeed.

The obvious solution was partition. Unacceptable to Asquith and the Irish, partition put Law in a difficult position. Partition might make the government appear less intransigent but meant abandoning the Southern Unionists who enjoyed considerable support in the party. Law's position was eased somewhat when Carson announced his support for partition. Law spoke in favour while making clear his conviction that ministers could not accept compromise.[13]

The government's majority fell to 69 on the Agar-Robartes amendment, which advocated exclusion but was defeated. Law's strategy remained intact. Nonetheless, Law did seem to leave open the door to compromise; *we will support any Amendment which, bad as the Bill seems to us to be, would make it less bad.* Law was not offering a compromise but expressing a willingness to consider one offered by the government. Ulster's exclusion was now on the agenda. A compromise offered by Unionists, Law believed, would encourage Asquith's belief that Law was bluffing. Law did not welcome civil war, neither did he drop his implacable hostility to Home Rule but if there was to be Home Rule it was incumbent on ministers to structure it to avoid civil war:

They know that Ulster is in earnest ... there are stronger influences than Parliament [sic] majorities. They know that in that case no Government would dare to use their troops to drive them out ... the Government which gave the order to employ troops for that purpose would run a greater risk of being lynched in London than the loyalists of Ulster would run of being shot in Belfast.[14]

This was the background to Law's best-remembered speech, the speech that subsequently defined his image. Buoyed up by two by-election victories and the solidarity of Ulster, Law travelled to yet another monster anti-Home Rule rally held at Blenheim Palace on 27 July. Law's speech reprised his well-honed analysis of the government's illegitimacy but went further in identifying what this meant for Unionists: *In our opposition to them we shall not be guided by the considerations, we shall not be restrained by the bonds, which would influence us in ordinary political struggle. We shall use any means to deprive them of the power which they have usurped and compel them to face the people who they have deceived. The main instrument of this would be the Protestant people of Ulster.*

Then came the most disturbing statement ever uttered by a British politician: *While I had still in the party a position of less responsibility than that which I have now I said that in my opinion if an attempt were made without the clearly expressed will of the people of this country, and as part of a corrupt Parliamentary bargain, to deprive these men of their birthright, they would be justified in resisting by all means in their power, including force. I said so then, and I say now, with a full sense of the responsibility which attaches to my position, that if the attempt be made under present conditions, I can imagine no length of resistance to which Ulster will go, in which I shall not be ready to support them, and in which they will not be supported by the overwhelming majority of the British people.*[15]

I can imagine no length of resistance to which Ulster will go, in which I shall not be ready to support them, and in which they will not be supported by the overwhelming majority of the British people

BONAR LAW

If Asquith could not be verbally bludgeoned into dissolution, could the King be persuaded to exercise the prerogative and force Asquith out? Law had to tread carefully. He had been advised by Dicey that the monarch's power to refuse to sign legislation was dead but the King's right to warn and advise remained as did other aspects of the prerogative, such as seeking alternative advice. The King, Law argued, had a duty to seek alternative sources of advice, particularly when great constitutional changes were proposed. The precedent was the 1832 Reform Act. Two elections had been fought on reform; bills had been passed by the Commons and then amended by the Lords. The King refused to create the peers necessary to override the Lords' veto and sent for the Leader of the Opposition and only when the Leader of the Opposition proved unable to form a government, the King agreed to create peers.

Pushing the King by forceful rhetoric into seeking alternative advice was fraught with constitutional and political dangers and there was no guarantee that even if the King agreed with Law he would follow this policy. The King, naturally concerned to avoid a runaway conflict, believed that the best solution was compromise. Law's first encounter with George V over Home Rule was at a State Dinner at Buckingham Palace in May 1912. Law drove home to the King his (Law's) interpretation of the political logic of Home Rule. Receiving the King's permission to speak freely, Law warned that *the situation is a grave one not only for the House but also for the Throne. Our desire has been to keep the Crown out of our struggles, but the Government have brought it in. Your only chance is that they should resign within two years. If they don't, you must either accept that Home Rule Bill or dismiss your Ministers and choose others who will support you in vetoing it – and in either case half your subjects will think you have acted against them.* Law piled on the pressure, *They* [ministers] *may argue that your assent* [to the Home Rule bill] *is a purely formal act and the prerogative of veto is dead. That was true as along as there was a buffer* [the House of Lords] *between you and the House of Commons, but they have destroyed the buffer and it is true no longer.*[16] Law planted doubt in the King's mind, which gradually flowered into a concern about the stability of the political system and monarchy.

Law had a second conversation with the King on 27 September, which he used to increase the King's nervousness. Law told the King that the Unionists regarded the Constitution as suspended; by-election losses had undermined the government's credibility and legitimacy. This, Law argued, *is precisely similar to what it would be if the Government supported by the House of Commons asked the Sovereign to use the Prerogative to overcome the opposition of the House of Lords.* The King's duty and constitutional right was, before acting on ministerial advice to assent to the bill, to try and find an alternative government (the 1832 precedent). The government, Law conceded, would insist the monarch was obliged to accept his minister's advice. However: *In reality it does not matter much which of these views is constitutionally sound. In any case whatever course was taken by HM half his people would think that he had failed in his duty & in view of the many bitter feelings which by that time would have been aroused the Crown would, Mr Bonar Law fears, be openly attached by the people of Ulster & their sympathisers if he gave his assent to the Bill & by a large section of the Radical Party if he took any other course.*[17]

Law doubted the King could or would veto the bill but he continued to believe that if ministers gave advice, which the King disapproved, he had the right and duty to see if different ministers would give him different advice. There was no problem with the King advising or seeking to persuade his Prime Minister that a general election was in the national interest. Infinitely more contentious was whether the Crown retained the *de facto* power to dismiss Asquith. Even if the power were deemed operative its use would be extremely dangerous. On 6 January 1913 the Home Rule bill passed the House of Commons and nine days later the House of Lords rejected it. The House of Commons needed to pass the bill only one more time and under the 1911 Act it would become law in mid-1914.

Asquith strongly advised the King that it was impossible for a constitutional monarch to do anything other than accept his ministers' advice. The most a monarch could do was formally and officially register dissent. Resolutely denying any possibility of confining an election to a single issue, Asquith hinted at special treatment for Ulster. Lansdowne reported to Law the King's enthusiasm for negotiations between ministers and the opposition. At Balmoral on 17 September Law expressed scepticism about exclusion without the approval of the Southern Unionists, without which exclusion would be seen by many as a cynical betrayal. Law reminded the King of the likely effect of Home Rule on the Army, doubting that the Army would coerce Ulster. At Balmoral Law had talked with Churchill whom Asquith had tasked with seeking a private meeting with Law. Conceding the situation was desperate, Law warned Churchill it was serious for the Liberals, stressing that the Army could not be relied on to enforce government policy. Unionists would support their refusing orders from an unconstitutional government.

Ulster's exclusion from Home Rule would raise issues of party management and possibly serious internal dissent. Exclusion was viable only if endorsed by the Southern Unionists. A second problem was that the King would pounce on exclusion as a compromise and Law's strategy to force an election would be in ruins. Moreover, Asquith, Law feared, might offer exclusion to provoke the Southern loyalists and English Unionists. By October Carson was reporting a significant shift in opinion: Southern Unionists would not seriously oppose Ulster's exclusion. This eased Law's doubts about meeting Asquith because it would limit the impact of Die-Hard hostility, which could be countered by an appeal to party unity and Ulster's rights. This would be acceptable to those, including the King, who were appalled by the prospect of civil war but would not be acceptable to Irish National-ist opinion. Those who would be scandalised at 'betraying' Southern Unionists were few but could cause a great deal of trouble.

Law and Asquith held three meetings (on 15 October, 6 November and 9 December) at Aitken's house. Law and

Asquith warily circled each other. Law admitted exclusion would remove one of the party's arguments for an election but the danger of a Die-Hard reaction remained. Asquith rejected an election, arguing that Ulster would resist Home Rule irrespective of any election result. If, however, Liberals won the election Law would not support Ulster's resistance. Neither Asquith nor Law could predict the future, so both could rationally pursue a strategy of intransigence. Asquith could not believe Law would not compromise on Ulster's exclusion; Law could not believe Asquith would risk civil war. Three options were discussed: Home Rule for Ulster; exclusion for a fixed period after which it would come under the authority of the Dublin Parliament; and exclusion with provision to join the rest of Ireland later if its population so wished. Law was dismissive. The Cabinet discussed exclusion followed by Ulster's inclusion after a certain period unless the Act was amended. This would never be acceptable to the Ulster Unionists or to Law and charges of betrayal were flying. Law believed Asquith had acted in bad faith. He interpreted Asquith's actions as an attempt to fix the responsibility for any breakdown on Law and Ulster's intransigence.

At Bristol (15 January) Law stated *so far as I can judge, there can be no result*, not because the government did not want a solution, but because they were prevented from so doing by the Irish MPs. He continued: *We think Home Rule a great evil, but we think that civil war is an evil infinitely greater, and if the Government could make to us any proposal which would do away with the prospect of civil strife ... we should be ready to consider it with a real desire to accept it* [but] *Any proposal which does not meet the claims, the just claims, of the people of Ulster, must be futile ... it will not prevent the outbreak of civil strife.* Law concluded, *they must appeal to the people.*[18] Despite a frosty reaction from the King Law gave no ground: without Ulster's unconditional exclusion and plausible safeguards for Southern Loyalists there could be no workable solution. Asquith's dependence on the Nationalists and pressure from the King, Law sensed, was leaving Asquith with a stark choice: an election or civil war. Law could not believe Asquith would choose the latter.

Law continued to try and manoeuvre Asquith into choosing *satisfying and conciliating Ulster*. Ulster's resistance had to be a credible threat. Thus, *if Ulster does resist ... until the matter is decided by the people ... we will support them*. However, if ministers *satisfy Ulster, automatically the danger of civil tumult disappears, and however wrong we may consider you are in pressing your proposals forward before you have submitted them to the country, you can carry them independently of us without any danger of civil strife*. Temporary exclusion postponed a final reckoning but if ministers accommodated Ulster they could count on his and the party's help on condition *that Ulster, or a part of Ulster, is not to be driven out of this Parliament while it wants to remain in it, and is not to be compelled to enter a National Parliament which it abhors, against the will of the people of Ulster*. If Asquith refused *it can only be because ... he prefers question be settled by bullets rather than votes*. If blood were shed the Army would shatter and *there will be precisely the same outburst of feeling here as that which took place in the United States when the first shot was fired at Fort Sumter*.[19]

The King refused to accept that compromise was impossible and that the only choice was an election or civil war. An election would not preserve the Crown's political neutrality, nor was it obvious how an election would resolve the Ulster question. If the Liberals won, Ulster would still fight, supported by many Unionists who would ignore Law's promise that the party would respect the result. The Unionist party would split to the advantage of the Liberal and the Labour parties. Most importantly, an election might become a 'King versus people' election: the Monarchy would be irretrievably politicised. The King, subject to massive countervailing pressure from Asquith, would not now insist on dissolution.

Law's intimidation of the government and King had failed. From this emerged the proposal to amend the Army Act to preclude its use in Ulster.[20] The Army Act had to be renewed each year otherwise a soldier would be in the same legal position as a civilian, and the structure of military discipline would be removed. If the government accepted the amendment it could not use the Army anywhere; if they rejected it, the Act would be in abeyance for two years under the terms of the Parliament Act. Law had previously expressed his support for this extremely dangerous and irresponsible strategy; he justified it on the familiar grounds that this was the only constitutional way to force an election. This was too much for many in the party and it was difficult to see how it could be presented positively to public opinion. The plan was abandoned on 20 March, the same day as the Curragh Incident. Asquith had concluded troops would have to be deployed to maintain law and order in Ulster and to protect military supplies. Officers stationed at the military camp at the Curragh outside Dublin were told that if they were unwilling to undertake operations in Ulster they would be permitted to resign their commissions. Fifty-seven officers of the 3rd Cavalry Brigade, commanded by General Hubert Gough, told Gough they would accept dismissal rather than march on Ulster. Some infantry officers later joined. Given the over-representation of Ulstermen in the officer corps and the conservatism of the military it is not surprising they enjoyed considerable sympathy throughout the Army. They received a written assurance they would not be used to coerce Ulster, although this was not the government's intention.

The day before the Curragh Incident Law spoke of the *collision of two forces which could not be easily reconciled, and neither which could be easily weakened.* Law expressed, somewhat disingenuously, his hope that *some way of escape would be found from a catastrophe which ... would be abhorrent to the great mass of opinion throughout the nation.* He could not, however, see a way out.[21] Law exploited the Curragh Incident: *nothing can save the Army now* – [Interruption] – *nothing can save the Army now except a clear declaration on the part of the government that officers will not be compelled* – [Hon. Members: 'And Men'] – *and men will not be compelled* – *to engage on civil war against their will.*[22]

On 24 April 35,000 Mauser rifles and three million rounds of ammunition for the Protestant Ulster Volunteer Force (UVF) were landed at Larne without any interference from the authorities. Leading Ulster Unionists organised the gunrunning, and although Law was deliberately kept in the dark, it was well known in Unionist circles what was afoot. Naturally sympathetic, Law as an elected politician condemned it as deplorable. Whether there was to be peace or war, Law insisted, was Asquith's personal responsibility but Law announced his willingness to explore possible solutions.[23] The Curragh and Larne episodes damaged Law but he still strove to provoke an election. Law had no scruples about exploiting the Curragh Incident to damage the government: *no majority, however large or in whatever way its worked, can get over the fundamental difficulties with which the Government is faced. The forces which are going to decide this question ... are not within these walls, but are outside, and that is due to the change of* [political] *system you have introduced.* The King would not intervene; Asquith would not call an election, leaving exclusion as Law's best remaining option: *the Government ... have the power ... to carry a Home Rule Bill which, by satisfying Ulster, will not create civil war. We have regarded civil war as the greatest of all possible calamities, and position has been, and is to-day, as strong as ever that if Home Rule can be carried in spite of us, we shall do everything in our power to make it easy for the Government to carry it without, rather than with, civil strife as a consequence.*[24] It would have to be crystal-clear what was being offered because neither the Unionists nor Ulster trusted the government.

By the end of April moves to explore compromise between Asquith and Law were underway. Law and Carson expressed their doubts that Asquith could compromise because of Redmond's opposition. Law and Carson believed the best means to proceed was an amending Bill introduced in the Lords (under Unionist control) which would receive the Royal Assent simultaneously with the original Home Rule bill. On 12 May Asquith announced that the third and final reading of the bill would take place before the Whitsun recess but promised to introduce an amending bill immediately after the break. Asquith was subject to a furious attack by Law who accused him of a serious breach of faith. Home Rule would pass the Commons with no guarantee other than the government's word that Ulster would be safeguarded. Asquith's majority ensured the proposal was carried.

After the recess the Unionists pressed for guarantees and a clear indication of what the government's exclusion proposals would be. Asquith refused. The result was uproar, which the Speaker could not quell. Losing his composure he asked Law directly whether the demonstration had his approval. Infuriated, Law coldly refused to answer and rebuked the Speaker. The possibility of a Die-Hard revolt in the party remained but with Law laying into the government and with the government's commitment to an amending bill on the agenda, few in the party were willing to threaten Law's position. Under this battering, Asquith, with the Home Rule bill passed by the Commons and subject to the Parliament Act, agreed to introduce the amending bill in the Lords on 23 June. Identical to the 8 March bill it proposed a separate option for each county to remain outside the Home Rule government for six years followed by automatic inclusion unless the Westminster parliament had in the meantime decided otherwise. The Unionists rejected it.

At the end of June and the beginning of July Asquith began serious attempts at compromise, partly because of the international situation. On 28 June the Archduke Franz Ferdinand was assassinated in Sarajevo. Law assumed there would be no county-by-county plebiscite but a new 'Protestant' area would be defined, the time limit would be abolished, Ulster would be allowed to determine its future. In return Law and Carson would acquiesce in Home Rule in the South and would not seek repeal. Negotiations agreed that Ulster would be excluded but could not agree on the position of Tyrone.

Asquith believed compromise was still possible and he asked the King to convene a conference. Law regarded this as another slippery move but the King's invitation would be impossible to refuse. The conference lasted from 21 to 24 July. Asquith and Lloyd George attended for the government, Law and Lansdowne for the Unionists, Redmond

> **John Edward Redmond** (1856–1918) had entered Parliament in 1881 as a supporter of the Irish nationalist leader Parnell and had continued to back him after the party split in 1890 over Parnell's divorce case scandal. When the two wings of the Irish Nationalist Party re-united in 1900, Redmond was accepted as their leader. Wedded to constitutional means to achieve Home Rule, Redmond worked to restrain extremists on his own side who armed in response to Carson's raising of the UVF. The Easter Rising of 1916 dashed all Redmond's hopes, and he died a broken man two years later.

and Dillon for the Nationalists, and Carson and Craig for the Ulster Unionists. The King, after welcoming the party leaders, played no further role. Speaker Lowther chaired proceedings. The main obstacle was Tyrone. Meeting for three sweltering days, they could find no solution. The government and the Nationalists appeared willing to give way on the time limit but could not say so openly until the excluded area had been defined. Carson and Craig would not surrender any part of Tyrone; nor would Redmond and Dillon. A compromise had to satisfy technical issues (what was to be excluded) and political questions (could it be sold to supporters), and neither Law nor Asquith could go slower or faster than their Irish parties would allow. Law had no expectation of success, although the Conference ended amicably.

The situation in Ulster continued to deteriorate. On 26 July an attempt by the nationalist Irish Volunteers to run guns in to the port of Howth in daylight miscarried. The authorities intervened, the police requested military support and in the ensuing unrest troops killed three civilians and wounded 38 more. Contrasting the inaction of the Army and police at the UVF's gunrunning, nationalist opinion hardened. Redmond, as a result of the furore, secured a delay in considering the Amending Bill in the Commons until 30 July. The bill was never discussed. On the day that the Buckingham Palace conference ended news was received of the Austrian ultimatum to Serbia, the rejection of which led to general mobilisation. On 4 August Britain declared war on Germany.

Chapter 5: War

Law's war can be divided into three phases: patriotic opposition (August 1914–May 1915), the First Coalition (May 1915–December 1916), and the Second Coalition (December 1916–November 1918). Law had no role in the determination of grand strategy. He of course had views on the war's conduct and his opinion, as on the Dardanelles, could be decisive. Like Lloyd George he felt ill-equipped to the challenge the Generals; unlike Lloyd George he never overcame his reticence but Law was central to the war's political management.[1] Law responded frequently to Unionist pressure for the vigorous prosecution of the war, acting to prevent power shifting to the back benches. His signal contribution was to provide Prime Ministers with a (more or less) reliable House of Commons. To this end he brought down one Prime Minister and created a second.

Law was the first to admit that foreign affairs were his weak spot. He had no basic quarrel with the direction of foreign policy, especially the entente with France that had originated with Balfour's government. Law was among those who hoped Britain could keep out of a Continental war but soon accepted this was impossible. His first speech on foreign affairs was during the Agadir Crisis of 1911 where he expressed the conviction that Germany and Britain should never go to war. The German invasion of Belgium, in violation of its treaty obligations, changed his position. *This*, he concluded, *is no small struggle. It is the greatest, perhaps, that this country has ever been engaged in, and the issue in uncertain. It is Napoleonism once again.*[2] Law gave ministers *the assurance on behalf of the party of which I am leader in this House, that in whatever steps they think it necessary to take for the honour and security of this country, they can rely on the unhesitating support of the Opposition.*[3]

During a national emergency Law believed opposition should be suspended. This, however, depended on a *quid pro quo*. On 30 July the government announced the postponement of the second reading of the Government of Ireland (Amendment) Bill that would exclude Ulster. Law feared a trick but nonetheless agreed. Domestic differences must be secondary to *us presenting a united front in the counsels of the world … in the meantime party controversial business will not be taken.*[4] The government's decision to proceed with Welsh Church disestablishment and the abolition of plural voting were, Unionists felt, 'controversial'. Infinitely more serious was Asquith's announcement on 15 September of his intention of putting the Home Rule Bill on the statute book with implementation delayed until after the war. The Carlton Club left Law in no doubt about party feelings. Law was icy in his condemnation. The government *took advantage of our patriotism to betray us* and t*hey are deliberately breaking pledges as solemn as were ever given to any Parliament by any Government.* In thrall to the Irish, Asquith was risking disruption of the war effort by his partisanship. The fault was Asquith's because *until that struggle is over, so far as we were concerned … there would be no party, there would only be a nation.*[5] Nevertheless, the Opposition would continue to aid the government. It had been agreed previously that only Law would speak: his MPs sat in stony silence. When he finished the Unionists rose and left the Chamber. Unionists felt betrayed: 'Asquith had behaved

like a card sharper and should never be received into a gentleman's house again'; 'They really are blackguards this Govt...
. they have calculated on our loyalty to our Country to play this dirty trick on us.'[6]

In January 1915 the Unionist Business Committee (UBC) was formed to articulate backbench frustration over the conduct of the war. Law and Asquith, albeit for different reasons, agreed the Unionists should play no formal role in government but Unionist disquiet, Law knew, was moving in favour of greater opposition not co-operation. This entailed the danger of a political crisis so severe that it could be resolved only by dissolution and Law resolutely opposed a wartime election. Coalition was inevitable as government incompetence became manifest but Law would not precipitate a crisis. This meant sustaining Asquith and restraining his backbenchers but the UBC was a sharp reminder of the limits under which he was operating. Critics argued Law's patriotic duty was to be critical, not to jeopardise the war effort but to improve the government's performance. Patriotic opposition operated to the government's advantage because Unionists remained silent, so ministers had no incentive to improve their performance. Ministers enjoyed all the advantages of coalition and none of its disadvantages. This was in the interests of neither the party nor the country and was unsustainable.

Law's starting-point was that Unionists should take no responsibility for the war's conduct. If ministers continued to be behave as in the recent past, however, *I am not at all sure that we should not openly declare that the truce is at an end, and tell them privately before any action is taken that this is the course that we shall adopt*. Law was also reluctant to seek more information about the war. With information came responsibility. Increased Unionist membership of the War Council, regarded by Law as an inner-cabinet, would be dangerously destabilising: *if their views were not carried out they would either have to allow things to go on for which they would be regarded as responsible; or, they would have to break away from the arrangement and make it public that they had done so.* Unionist members would brief colleagues and there would be inevitable differences that could not be kept secret. Law conceded the *status quo* was unsatisfactory but *we are conducting the most difficult war ... in regard to which the nation is united, but half the nation distrusts the men who are carrying it on.* Lurking in any controversy was a potential party split, so, *much as I dislike the present position, there are I think only two real alternatives open to us: One is to go on as we are doing, without responsibility and with very limited amount of criticism ... or to face a coalition.* Hostile to coalition, *I am reluctantly driven to the conclusion that the only proper course for us in the meantime is to continue on the lines on which we have acted since the war began.*[7] Law hinted that rejection of his policy would mean resignation, his strategy during the referendum crisis.

Despite the nature of the fighting, the organisation of production by the War Office under Kitchener failed to keep pace. The failure of the British offensive at Neuve Chapelle (10–13 March) and heavy casualties at the Second Battle of Ypres were blamed in part by *The Times* on a shortage of shells. The Shells Crisis led Conservative backbenchers to focus on the government's, rather than Kitchener's, failings. Another failure occurred at Aubers Ridge (18–25 May), while the Dardanelles expedition proceeded inexorably towards disaster after the failed attempt to force the Straits in March and the bloody landings at Gallipoli on 25 April. The political sands were shifting. Unionist MPs and some Liberals (notably Lloyd George) were unhappy with the central direction of the war and with Home Rule on the statute books Irish Nationalists had less reason to support Asquith. Possible conscription in Southern Ireland made Irish support increasingly conditional. Unionist disquiet exploded. Law and Lansdowne told Maurice Hankey, the Cabinet Secretary, that 'it would be impossible for them, for party reasons, to attend [the war council] in future. If they did so they feared it would weaken their position in the Conservative Party and, as [Law] put it, render their future support of the government less effective.'[8] UBC criticism of the war's direction deeply worried Law. A debate on the conduct of the war could run out of control and even if the government won, a serious blow would be dealt the government, and a substantial hostile Unionist vote would damage Law.

Opposition had no role at this point in nation's history, nevertheless, *I am getting constantly criticised by my own friends … because we do not criticise the Government enough. Where are we to draw the line? My experience in the House is that you cannot have sham fights. Once you begin, it is very difficult to draw the line.*[9] All that concerned Law was the production of sufficient munitions and he contrasted the 'push and go' of Lloyd George with Asquith's complacency. The problem was a lack of central direction, which was Asquith's fault: *He* [Asquith] *had appointed plenty of Committees, and if Committees would end the War it would have ended long ago.* Law hinted that without radical change, the government's days were numbered: *I do not think that any Government that ever existed could have survived if there had been a really hostile Opposition finding fault with everything that they did.* Law was not calling for Asquith's removal but for greater energy and the involvement of technocrats in organising the war effort. Law eloquently expressed the Unionist dilemma, and, whatever his proclaimed intention,

He [Asquith] had appointed plenty of Committees, and if Committees would end the War it would have ended long ago.

BONAR LAW

issued a public warning that Unionist patience and forbearance had limits.

Less than a month later, Law and the Unionists were in government with Asquith. The Dardanelles precipitated the crisis. On 14 May the War Cabinet resolved to transfer ships from the Grand Fleet to the Eastern Mediterranean but Admiral Fisher, the First Sea Lord, objected and on 15 May he resigned. Fisher, like Kitchener, was popular with Unionist MPs, unlike his boss Winston Churchill. Law was willing to force Churchill out but not Asquith, nor would he countenance a fight between Asquith and his backbenchers, and he concluded patriotic opposition had outlived its usefulness. On 17 May Law saw Lloyd George at the Treasury and they agreed the only way to avoid a parliamentary crisis was to broaden the government. Lloyd George went to Number 10 to see Asquith who agreed, Lloyd George then collected Law, returned to Number 10 and the first coalition was formed. Law moved for three reasons: he was close to losing control of his party; the country was teetering on the brink of full-scale party conflict; and if this occurred there was a serious danger of a destabilising wartime election. Coalition was Law's least bad option as indeed it was for Asquith who remained Prime Minister, but the real winner was Lloyd George who increased his status and power by becoming Minister of Munitions. On 18 May Unionist leaders approved Law's decisions and the coalition was announced.

Asquith and Law were equally at pains to emphasise the coalition's limited purpose: *what is the best method of finishing the war successfully*. Law's demeanour testified to his lack of enthusiasm and he was greeted by cries of 'Speak Up'. A Coalition, Law emphasised, meant *our convictions on other subjects will remain unchanged and will be settled when this danger is over.*[10] Averting threats to his leadership and the war effort meant the Unionists could not form a government without a general election because neither Liberals, Labour nor the Irish would serve under Law. Law forced Churchill from the Admiralty but the Liberals resented sharing power and Asquith was determined to limit Unionist influence. That many Unionists regarded Asquith as an incompetent drunkard, though this was not Law's view, hardly improved relations. Unionists felt Law had been out manoeuvred in the distribution of spoils. Law might have claimed the Treasury or Ministry of Munitions but believed Lloyd George was best suited to the latter and Asquith refused to appoint a tariff reformer to the Treasury. Actually, he did not want three Conservatives at the War Office (he counted Kitchener as a Unionist), the Admiralty, or Munitions. Law accepted reluctantly the backwater of the Colonial Office after, according to Davidson, an impassioned plea from Lloyd George urging him 'not to put party or personal ambition in front of his patriotic duty and the unity of the new Government'. This was finely calculated to appeal to Law's sensibilities but he remained bitter. This drove a wedge between Law and Lloyd George and convinced Asquith that Law was a second-rater who could be discounted.[11]

This was a dangerous game for Asquith. Law had, after all, made one coalition and Asquith did not appreciate his attitude weakened Law's authority with his own party. This could make Law, and the coalition, vulnerable to the right. Law could have demanded more and senior posts but did not do so solely out of patriotism. Law was not naive, he was well aware of his and the party's centrality to the coalition. *You mustn't think*, Beaverbrook reports Law saying, *I am doing this because I am compelled to. I know very well I can have what I want simply by lifting my little finger. But I won't fight. I am here to show you how to run a Coalition Government by forbearance and concession.*[12]

The most serious threat to Asquith was a Law–Lloyd George alliance. LG's mistress noted Asquith's efforts to drive a wedge between them by telling LG Law wanted to be Leader of the House. By November 1915 Law was deeply unhappy with the coalition's direction. His exclusion by Asquith from the War Cabinet was 'A nasty slap in the face [but] he can't resign now because it will be attributed to pique ... So he must defer it for a bit and share the odium ... before his chance of jumping ashore comes again.'[13] The fall-out from the Dardanelles began the slide. Law and LG were convinced the peninsula should be evacuated. Unionist ministers were divided and the stability of the coalition and Law's leadership was threatened by Carson's resignation from the government on 15 October. This made Carson the leader of the Unionist opposition. On 31 October General Munro, the commander on the ground, recommended evacuation provoking an internal crisis (3–4 November), Asquith prevaricated by asking Kitchener to report. Reluctant to openly challenge Asquith and force the military's hand Law agreed to Kitchener's mission and then changed his mind. On 7 November Law met Asquith at Asquith's request and Law made it clear that unless the Dardanelles was evacuated

Field Marshal Earl Kitchener (1850–1916) was the most famous soldier in Britain in 1914. Appointed Secretary of State for War when war was declared, he, unlike many, understood that it was going to be a long war requiring a mass army, which he initially sought to raise through a call for volunteers, which succeeded beyond all expectations. However, his lack of administrative and political experience meant he was gradually sidelined by the rest of the government. Stripped of control of strategy in 1915, he went on a mission to Russia in 1916, but was drowned when the cruiser he was aboard hit a mine off the Orkneys.

he would resign. On 23 November the government agreed to evacuation.

In the House of Commons Law defended the government whilst making his disquiet clear. Although he had *taken no part in any of the general discussions of the policy of the Government* and was *the Leader of the largest party in this House under peculiar circumstances*, these circumstances lead him to defend an unpopular government. Stating that governments should be judged by their success and that *the real test is whether it is the fault of the Government that victories do not come*, Law was inviting critics to judge the government. They found it wanting, and he agreed with the critics that *the Coalition Government has not succeeded as well – I will not say as I expected, but as well as I hoped*, but the mechanisms of vigorous opposition and an election were unavailable. There was no alternative to the Coalition, which was imperfect. Law admitted the war's central direction was wanting. He wanted *some smaller body entrusted with special Executive action* and he criticised *the tendency … to magnify every little success and to hide every failure*.[14] They were conducting an experiment whose success partly depended on the cohesion and unity of Parliament, he concluded.

In late 1915 a bill was proposed to extend the life of the 1910 Parliament and avoid an election in December 1915 and ministers included in this the abolition of plural voting. Unionist ministers acquiesced reluctantly, their MPs objected violently to abolition. This was 'controversial' legislation and proof of Liberal duplicity and, more seriously, of the flaccidity of their leaders. Once again Law had to defend the Coalition and his stewardship. He admitted the abolition of plural voting had caused him problems. There were limits to non-party sentiments: *at the time this Coalition was formed we as a party made … the biggest party sacrifice which a political party can ever make … we abandoned what we believed to be the prospect of getting office ourselves*. Asquith was wrong to bring forward plural voting but Law then put the government's case. His motivation was to avoid any quarrel that might undermine the war effort and whilst there might come a time when Asquith wanted the Unionists, or the Unionists wanted, to leave the government but they would not leave on a party issue. He reminded Unionists *you cannot be half in and half out of a Government*. Law acknowledged that the Coalition *has not been a great success, but it has not been a great failure* and it would not be successful *if it means only that half a dozen Unionists are in the government and the Unionist party is against the Government*. Law concluded by making their continued participation dependent on Unionist opinion; *if the party to which I belonged showed that it had lost confidence in me I should not for a moment dream of continuing in the Government*. This would also mean he would leave the leadership.[15] Opponents agreed not to oppose the second reading, concluding 'the moral seems to be that we have got to agree with Govt. [*sic*] or give in when we don't'. Law's speech had a considerable positive effect; 'It was certainly his frankness that took everyone's breath away; but I think Squiff & co. must have felt rather uncomfortable.'[16] Unionists remained restive, grumbling about their lack of influence. This culminated in the political crisis of December 1916 on which so much ink has been expended. On 8 November 1916 a debate about the sale of German assets in Nigeria ran out of control. The government proposed to sell to the highest bidder; an amendment sought to confine the sale to British interests. Carson used the opportunity to launch an assault on the government. This was an extremely bad-tempered debate in which Carson virtually accused the government of a want of patriotism, of displaying contempt for the House and public opinion, and a lack of enthusiasm in prosecuting the war. Law, as the responsible minister, responded in kind. Law accused Carson and his supporters of irresponsibility and irrationality. He concluded, *I am sorry, very sorry to be so much at variance with my hon. Friends opposite, but the conditions under which the government is carried on produce strange results All that any of us can do is... what we believe best for the one objective we all have in view.*[17] The Unionist vote, nominally 286, split 65 for Carson and 73 for the government, with 117 for the amendment and 231 against. Shocked by the vote, Law believed both himself and the government in a potentially devastating situation that could only be resolved by a dissolution or reconstruction. As the former was unthinkable, reconstruction was the only viable strategy. The Nigeria Debate was the final straw. The December crisis was straightforward: both Law and LG lost any remaining confidence in Asquith's management of the war and to avoid the government falling and the Unionist party splitting, Asquith had to go. In the political conditions of late 1916 there was only one viable prime minister and that was Lloyd George and Law was to put him in Number 10.

The war fostered issues of consent and legitimacy different in degree and content than before 1914. Problems of mass consent and legitimacy mesmerised political elites, leading bemused politicians to ponder the configuration of post-war politics. The war's political impact flowed from its mass character: production required the co-operation of organised labour, the men suffering in the trenches and the women working in the factories could not be denied the vote, and the pre-war party system was fragmenting. These developments prompted questions not answers. Was the Liberal split temporary? How influential would labour – organised and political – be? Looming over this was Lloyd George. Would he form a centre party? Lloyd George reciprocated Conservative suspicion. Lloyd George never doubted Law and the Conservatives would support him as PM but they 'would still be distrustful of him; and rightly too, he says, for his ideals are not theirs, & he hates their régime & their policy, & always will …'.[18] Law's importance was reflected in his appointments, both Chancellor of the Exchequer and Leader of the House. He was 'minister for the home front' and remembering Law's role over the Dardanelles, Lloyd George was careful to square him on strategic issues and met him for two hours every day. LG carried an enormous burden physically, politically and emotionally and relied on Law: 'He possessed real courage. It was not the blind dash of the reckless or the buoyant courage of the sanguine. He anticipated trouble everywhere and everytime, and mostly exaggerated it. Nevertheless, he faced it without flattering if it came. He was both fearless and apprehensive. His great phrase in beginning and ending an interview was "There is lots of trouble ahead!"'[19]

With so mercurial a figure as Lloyd George Law's dourness was valuable. Law's 'greatest work was necessarily negative. It was what he prevented being done rather than what he did himself … had it not been for the countervailing influence of Bonar Law the vessel might, on more than one occasion, have capsized.'[20] The way the two complemented one another was often noted: 'If George's vision and drive could have been combined with Law's business habits and straightness, the results would have been doubled.'[21]

As Chancellor Law believed as much of the war effort as possible should be financed by current revenue but feared the long-term legacy of high direct taxation. Law thought some of LG's proposed tax increases, for example, too high: 'Very well', was [LG's] reply. 'If you oppose them, I shall withdraw them. But remember, the responsibility for dealing with this question will then rest with you!' LG was exploiting Law's reluctance to accept responsibility for policy (and Law knew this); equally, both Law and LG knew the latter needed the former's support, so far from manipulating Law these consummate politicians were negotiating. 'In the end he agreed that if the taxes were considerably reduced, his party would support them. [LG] quite willing to agree to this, having put them up especially high in anticipation of having to reduce them.'[22] Taxation is one reason why Law wanted the Treasury and insisted on it in 1916. The scale of the war changed Law's mind. He felt *the burden of taxation already extremely heavy, and, however necessary it may be, no one can doubt that in whatever form that taxation is raised, it diminishes the capital that may be available at the end of the War ... it is a handicap upon trade after the War.* Deeper motivations for Law's efforts to hold down direct taxation was retaining working class and trade union support for the war. The war was an opportunity: *the recovery of this country after the War will depend on the use we make of the new methods and the new machinery ... and will depend above all upon the extent to which the old hostility between capital and labour can be removed, so that both can work together to get the best possible output in the national interest.*[23]

This linked to a major theme in his second budget speech: the shifting balance of global financial power. By 1918 the UK had loaned its allies £505 million and borrowed £500 million from the United States. What concerned Law were the consequences of the absurdity of *borrowing with one hand, while we are lending with the other.* Law feared, with good reason, that the pattern of international borrowing with the USA at the centre of a complex web threatened massive post-war turbulence. Hence the need to ensure the economy's post-war vitality. There was an obvious political dimension to Law's concern with financial stability: *it is absolutely essential that we should not levy taxation on such a scale as to cripple every industry and every financial institution in this country ...* Wartime taxation was bound to be more severe than peacetime but in both cases: *Nothing could be worse than to put taxation on any class on a scale which seems to them in excess of the needs of the situation. For that reason we really must be moderate in the amount which we raise by taxation* ...[24]

Law's budgets are important for the concern displayed about post-war political-economic problems and mass consent. Determined to restrain high direct taxation Law feared the political realities of mass democracy would check this. A stable post-war political economy would be helped by an increase in the power and status of the Treasury in economic management. Liberal governance had fatally undermined the self-regulating pre-1914 system, which, though attractive and desirable as an ideal, was no longer feasible. The Bank of England, as guardian of this system, was inadequate to the task. The Cunliffe episode provided further proof of Law's killer instinct and secured Treasury dominance. In July 1917 Lord Cunliffe, the Bank's governor since 1913, reversed Law's instruction that £17 million in gold deposited in Canada be put at the disposal of Sir Herman Lever in New York to support various financial operations. Cunliffe ordered the gold transferred instead to J.P. Morgan & Co. Demanding an explanation, Law was told by Cunliffe to, in effect, mind his own business. Law demanded LG's support, telling him to choose between his Chancellor and his Bank governor. Soon after Cunliffe retired.

The Leader of the House's task is to deliver a majority for the PM. Law had to do this by accommodating Unionists to LG's political needs. A good example of this was Churchill's return to politics as Minister of Munitions. After front-line service Churchill returned to politics and became a 'problem' and by May 1917 LG concluded it was safer to have him inside the government. Sacking Churchill had been a Unionist condition for supporting LG so his return to office annoyed many who regarded Churchill as a dangerous maniac. Law was in a difficult position. LG appointed Churchill without consulting Law leaving him with a choice: acceptance or resignation. At an UBC meeting on 19 July Law suppressed his annoyance, making clear, however, his conviction that a PM had the right to appoint his government. He had decided to support the PM; if repudiated by the meeting he would resign. Churchill's return, the prospect of defeat in 1917, war weariness, and LG's conflicts with the Generals convinced Law he must confront the party's discontents.

On 30 November 1917 the party met in conference for the first time since 1913. This proved a significant episode for both Law and British Conservatism. The meeting held at the Kingsway Hall was open only to party officers, the parliamentary party and constituency representatives. Law spent much of it answering questions. He conceded there was widespread disquiet in the party and that, once again, its interests had been sacrificed. Law insisted the party had been right to support Asquith and he had been right to try and reconcile LG and Asquith because *I am convinced that Unionist Government during the war will never get as much unity in the nation as is possible to a Government of another character supported by the Unionist Party*. Law made it clear that the Unionists' duty was to support the Prime Minister.[25] When this proved impossible he put Unionist weight behind LG.

The November-December Crisis brought LG to power and the created the modern premiership; 1916 is critical for the development of British politics. The post-1911 crisis paled alongside that of 1916–17, which was all the more destabilising because it was unexpected and was outside politicians' experience. During the conscription crisis C P Scott, editor of the *Manchester Guardian*, asked Law if an election or martial law was justified if there was organised resistance to compulsion. Fully briefed by MI5 on the state of public opinion Law, sensitised to the complexities of the politics of consent, feared precipitate action would split the country and Coalition. Law was, Scott noted, 'prepared to make all possible concessions in regard to safeguards against the compulsion of labour in order to win back the adherence of the Labour party and to retain its representatives in the Government.'[26] Law's determination to support Asquith and preserve the Coalition led to direct conflict with his party. The beneficiary was Carson. With LG and the Unionists favouring universal service (eventually imposed on 2 May) Law feared the Coalition would split and fall. Observers describe Law as in a state of acute indecision: LG 'says he has never seen anyone in such a state of abject funk. [BL] does not know which way to turn or what to do', and if LG resigned 'it is almost impossible for B.L. to stay in without being an object of contempt; & yet he is loath to resign.'[27] Law's 'indecision' was the consequence of an appreciation of what was at stake and that decisions taken now would reverberate in politics for decades.

Law's strategy was based on three elements: the fall of the Coalition might lead to a general election, this would seriously damage the war effort, and lead to an explosion of partisan conflict. Whilst he remained convinced of this, then the *status quo* was his least worst option. As the *status quo* was Asquith's best option, they were *de facto* allies. If Law became convinced that the Coalition could not be reformed under Asquith but that it could under another PM, this outcome would beat the *status quo*. Law did not want to be PM and while LG was not trusted, the *status quo* won. Law and LG had common ground: the need for compulsion the need to avoid unrest in Ireland after the Easter Rising in Dublin, and Kitchener's replacement at the War Office (WO). Law supported LG's appointment to the WO. Too late Asquith tried to split them, offering the WO to Law who refused. This increased further Law's disquiet over Asquith and reinforced his conviction of LG's importance to the war effort. This period was critical for Law personally and politically, coming down in favour of Lloyd George. Through 1916 Law believed the political base for a new government existed neither in Parliament nor the country. Now he changed his mind.

Asquith returned from Dublin in the aftermath of the Easter uprising convinced that only Home Rule could prevent further unrest. Law was willing to permit LG to try and find an agreement acceptable to Carson and Redmond. The compromise – Home Rule for the 26 counties with the six Ulster counties remaining part of the UK with a final solution to be discussed by a post-war Imperial conference – was (initially) acceptable to Carson and Redmond. Law believed this was the best likely deal and 'thinks everyone must see that a settlement which permanently excludes Ulster is a gain for Unionists. I suggest that a settlement, as a reward for rebellion, which gives the rebels much of what they ask for is not likely to please all our party.' Long, Lansdowne and Selbourne (who was to resign) and 80 MPs were hostile, particularly to the abandoning of the Southern Loyalists. Law's concern had always been Ulster and new realities, such as the need to reassure American opinion and the steady of erosion of Redmond's moderate nationalism by Sinn Fein, suggests Law now regarded Southern Unionism as a lost cause. At the Carlton Club on 7 July Unionist opinion, whilst resenting their treatment, nonetheless 'regard the breaking up of the Coalition as a disaster of sufficient magnitude to outweigh all other considerations, even broken pledges'.[28]

Law insisted LG's proposal was the best available. Rejection might lead to a Unionist government trying to govern Ireland

and Law recognised that English opinion would not understand a Die-Hard response especially as Ulster's position was guaranteed. The party acquiesced when Carson spoke in favour. This damaged Law and forced him to reassert his authority in the Nigeria debate and at the party conference. In response to a question why conscription had not been extended to Ireland, Law confessed this was an imperfect world: *rightly or wrongly, we came to the conclusion that from the point of view of the war we would lose more than we would gain by enforcing it now.* Ireland would be governed and sufficient forces would be kept in Ireland to prevent disorder. However, it was neither possible nor desirable to arrest Sinn Fein's leaders and *We believe that nothing – or very few things – would be a greater misfortune than to have the Irish question in its old form with unrestricted coercion.*[29]

On conscription Law trod a similar path: *even if we got a large majority the war would have to be carried on in the face of a bitter Opposition in the House of Commons which would ... encourage every form of Opposition outside. This might mean ... that something like martial law would have to be established in many parts of the country ... it is a risk so great that we should not be justified in facing it unless we were absolutely driven to it.* Law believed the army had little difficulty in recruitment as opposed to equipping the recruits and as with Ireland the main issue was consent. Labour's ministers *told me in the most emphatic way that if compulsion were extended now it would be impossible for them to carry any considerable section of the Labour movement in favour of it, and not only would it be necessary for them to resign but they felt sure there would be hostility of the most violent kind to the proposal by most of the trade unions of the country.*[30] Popular suspicion would fade but if the Unionists, led by Carson and prompted by the Generals, forced the issue the resulting crisis that might force the country out of the war.

Politics were changing. Law would, for example, have

preferred to defer consideration of the franchise bill until after the war. However, the mass nature of the war meant ministers had no choice: *Once we had the whole nation practically fighting for us, it was obvious that these men must have votes.* Once this was conceded there was no logical reason to exclude women and war workers and he concluded, *our Party if it is properly conducted has no reason to fear that the mass of the people of this country will not support it. If we cannot win that support, we may as well go out of business and it is our duty now at all events to make the best of the situation which has arisen and to see that everything is done by us to make our Party what Disraeli once called it – and what, if it is to have any existence, it must be – a really national Party.*[31] Class was replacing Home Rule as Conservatism's central concern.

Once we had the whole nation practically fighting for us, it was obvious that these men must have votes.

BONAR LAW

The 'old' politics refused to die, however. Ireland exploded back into politics as a consequence of the March 1918 German offensive that increased demand for manpower. Ministers contemplated the extension of conscription to Ireland, an extremely contentious proposition. In 1917 LG, largely as a sop to US opinion, had offered the Irish the 1916 deal once more. Redmond, being outflanked by Sinn Fein, could not accept. Those imprisoned after the 1916 rebellion were released and LG established a Convention in Dublin to search for a solution. However, Sinn Fein refused to participate and Carson and Ulster retained their veto. LG had sidelined Carson, who had backed the wrong side in the dispute over the convoy system, by 'promoting' him to the War Cabinet. Never really happy except in opposition, Carson resigned at the end of 1917. The Convention staggered on until the spring of 1918 when both Sinn Fein and the Ulster

Unionists rejected its proposals. Carson, out of office, was hovering in the wings. On 25 March the Cabinet agreed to extend conscription to Ireland. Law's position remained that of 1914, modified by 1916. Law would accept Home Rule if the Southern Unionists were protected (which he knew he could not secure) and Ulster was excluded (which he could), and argued that until a bill was ready, nothing precipitate should be done.

Carson believed Irish conscription would cause more trouble than that it was worth as Sinn Fein was dominant in the South and the Catholic hierarchy was urging resistance to conscription. LG's proposal to link conscription to Home Rule satisfied no one; the Nationalists left Westminster and threw in with Sinn Fein. Once again, Ireland threatened to disrupt the Coalition and the Unionist party but the US Army and the weakening of the German offensive saved both. The Allied counter-offensive shifted political attention to post-war strategy.

Chapter 6: Coalition and Post-War Conservatism

Always attracted by the lure of the centre, by late 1917 Lloyd George was contemplating creating a centre party led by himself. This could only be achieved by absorbing Conservative MPs (i.e. splitting the party), merging them with his own MPs and with Patriotic Labour and along the way possibly challenging and depriving Law of the leadership. As 'the man who won the war' with a populist appeal attractive to the non-socialist working class, LG appealed to Conservative voters as a source of stability. If the centre party idea worked, the main beneficiaries would be LG and Labour. Law had been warned that he ought, as leader of the Unionist party, to give some thought to the shape of post-war politics. Until May 1918 Law was not in a position to respond without confronting LG's political ambitions and thereby destabilising the Coalition.

In March 1918 LG and Law began discussions on electoral co-operation. By July a plan had emerged. LG and Law would allocate constituencies to LG's supporters and Coalition candidates would be endorsed, the famous 'Coupon'. These talks were kept secret from the party but Law was convinced the party had to co-operate with LG. Law had concluded *our Party on the old lines will have no future in the life of this country*. The main threat was *the extreme Labour Party* and challenging it required a truly national leader. Law did not believe himself qualified but noted *In the past we have suffered tremendously, because we have always had the whole of organised Labour against us. It is that that defeated our Tariff Reform proposal – that and that alone.* Labour was on the verge of splitting between patriotic and extreme wings. The party should work with *the section of Labour which is national and imperialistic*, this would change the party's aims and *we will have to pay the price.* However, *the Conservative Party has been a good thing for this country and it is our business today, and as long as we can, to keep that Party solid, and if splits must come, to delay them as long as we possibly can.*[1]

The government's victory in the Maurice Debate in May 1917 cemented the 1916 split: 71 Liberals supported LG and 98 Asquith. Law had been alarmed by LG but *now he knew him very well, he realised what magnificent qualities he had … and refused the role of trying to drive as hard a bargain for his party as he could.*[2] Twenty-four hours after the Armistice LG announced a general election. At a meeting of the Unionist parliamentary party, candidates and Central Council at the Connaught Rooms on 17 November, Law recommended the Coalition's continuation under LG and outlined the agreed policy. This was approved unanimously. The manifesto declared, 'The principle concern of every Government must be the condition of the great mass of the people who live by manual toil' and the government would deal 'on broad and comprehensive lines' with housing, education and labour standards. It promised a more protectionist industrial policy during the post-war transition. The election was a catastrophe for the independent Liberals. Asquith was defeated and only 28 Asquithians survived compared to 133 Coalition Liberals. The beneficiaries were the Conservatives, Labour and Sinn Fein.

In 1918 Law moved from Bootle to Glasgow. He campaigned little because of a mild attack of 'flu. Between

November 1918 and March 1921 Law was, as Leader of the House, at the centre of the government. He remained deputy PM, running the government and chairing the Cabinet while LG was at Versailles and other conferences. In Cabinet Law always sat on LG's left. As leader of the biggest party he was LG's political base and as LG attended the House infrequently so Law's statements were authoritative. Despite his exhaustion he was effective and adopted more emollient style than in the past, working hard to keep the House's confidence. In a time of political and electoral flux Conservatives had no option other than to co-operate with LG to retain moderate working class opinion whilst blocking LG's efforts to capture the centre-ground. Law felt the coalition's majority was *far too big to be wholesome*.[3] Whips would have to spend an inordinate amount of time managing a Coalition that, he feared, would unravel. This was compounded by an influx of new MPs (Baldwin's 'hard-faced men … who look as if they had done well out of the war') and Labour, now committed by its 1918 constitution to socialism, represented a far more serious threat than pre-war Radicalism.

Abroad, the Hohenzollern, Habsburg, Ottoman and Romanov imperial dynasties collapsed and a new colossus, the United States, emerged. Within the Empire disintegrative forces were at work, notably in Ireland and India. By the end of 1919 LG had accepted that the Coalition was unstable. He sought a 'National Democratic Party' because there 'is no enthusiasm for this coalition. The two party machines do not really co-operate … the field is left clear for the Bolshevists, Independent Labour Party, and the Labour Party.'[4] By March 1920 fusion as an anti-socialist device was supported by many politicians but it would give LG a party. Law regarded fusion as a necessary evil. LG and Law agreed to test party opinion but Coalition Liberal ministers rejected fusion, which meant Law avoided conflict with his party. Law remained concerned at being outflanked from the right by his own Die-Hards, from the left by Labour with, perhaps, LG developing a centrist-populism. 1918, the failure of fusion and the Coalition's fall offered the opportunity to create a mass anti-socialist Conservative Party. By 1922 the Conservatives dominated the middle class vote and were winning 25–30 per cent of the working class vote, and so between November 1918 and October 1922 Law's attitude to Coalition shifted dramatically.

For much of the middle class the period 1918–23 was one of deep and genuine crisis.[5] A fall in middle-class living standards was coupled with frustrated expectations and status panic but by 1923 the post-war crisis was resolved in their favour. These middle-class groups were central to the party's organisation and its core vote. They could not be ignored; equally they could not determine policy. Middle-class fury, articulated by the *Daily Express* and *Daily Mail*, focussed on profiteers, Jews, the working class and above all the organised working class. Equating the working class with the unions was not one the party could afford to make.

This conjunction was avoided by making the middle class the cornerstone of the 'constitutional classes', which could, and did, embrace the unorganised working class, the political expression of which was the Conservative Party. Under Law, 'defence of the middle class therefore, became defence of the constitution and the rights of the public; and the Conservative Party became the party of the public because it was the party of the constitution.'[6] Law was regarded as 'the businessman's friend'. Law did not believe that the state could confront union militancy without public support or material preparations. Law had made it clear in the House of Commons, in reference to a miners' strike, that *if the strike comes, it is not like an ordinary strike; it would not be a strike of wage-earners against their employers ... It would, if it comes, be a strike against the community ... If such a strike comes the Government – and no Government could do otherwise – will use all the resources of the State without the smallest hesitation ... We shall – and no Government could do otherwise – use all the resources of the State to win, and to win quickly ... if such a struggle comes it can only have one end, or there is an end to Government in this country.*[7]

All weapons ought to be available for distribution to the friends of the Government.

BONAR LAW

With the Emergency Powers Act of 1920, the creation of the Organisation for the Maintenance of Supplies and a politically reliable army and police force, confrontation became possible. To LG's amusement, at a conference on industrial conflict, ministers, including Law, appeared to panic. Law believed *All weapons ought to be available for distribution to the friends of the Government*, while another minister 'pointed to the Universities as full of trained men who could co-operate with clerks and stockbrokers. (During the discussion Bonar Law so often referred to the stockbrokers as a loyal and fighting class until one felt that potential battalions of stockbrokers were to be found in every town).'[8]

The re-stabilisation of society was not easy, nor was working class subordination total but in the face of intense middle class bitterness towards the unions what was achieved was remarkable. The vehicle for achieving this was the Conservative Party, which, Law implied in 1917, was in a position to appeal to the expanding middle class and the upwardly mobile aspirant working class in the new consumer goods and light industries. Both feared socialism and union militancy but in 1920–1 the working class was forced on to the defensive, its subordination being sealed by recession, unemployment and defeat in 1926. The City, industry and the party were united in their concern about the Coalition's inflationary tendencies – high taxes, expensive social welfare programmes and generous wage settlements – and favoured deflation. His economic orthodoxy meshed with party management on taxation: both had implications for foreign policy. He was convinced that current rates of confiscatory taxation had to be reduced if unemployment was to be tackled. These had to be accompanied by spending cuts even in the party's sacred cows, such as the Royal Navy because *there would be no world war for a very long time to come*. The foundation of Britain's strength was financial stability without which Britain could not defend its vital interests so *everything which human foresight and energy can do should be to keep our expenditure at the lowest level*.[9] The end of the post-war boom, the Cunliffe committee on monetary policy, the Geddes spending 'axe', and the Treasury's 'dear money' policy benefited those who gained from deflation and penalised those (the organised working class) that benefited from inflation. Deflation was presented as a moral, as much as a political or economic, good demanding responsible conduct from the state and individual. Its great symbol was the return to normality.

Labour posed the most serious medium-term threat to the Coalition but survival depended on Unionist loyalty so the immediate threat came from the Unionist right. The Die-Hard appeal – 'nationalist … anti-socialist and inegalitarian' – attracted the party's apparatus and many of its voters.[10] Though small in numbers (about 24 MPs) Die-Hards had the ability to inflame Unionists because many were seriously concerned about social reform, centralised government, government spending and debt, taxation and foreign adventurism. This disruptive ability can be seen in, for example, the Aliens Restriction Bill (23 October 1919) where the nay vote of 185 contained 120 Unionists and the vote on the Amritsar Massacre (8 July 1920) when 129 Unionists voted against the Coalition. By 1920 right-wing protest was gathering pace.

Pressure was building for a return to party politics and government. Compared to 1914, however, different issues dominated politics that required a 'national' approach and coalition reflected the electorate's preferences; *they hate extremes ... they chose the middle way.* The Coalition's justification was *that we are looking at each problem as it arises on its merits, without regard to party prejudice or party feeling, and that the one desire is to solve it in the best interests of the nation.*[11] The Anti-Waste Movement (founded in January 1921), blaming the nation's ills on government profligacy, union militancy and foreign adventurism, attracted many in the middle class. When Law resigned in March 1921 Anti-Waste was capturing Coalition seats in the South; Labour was doing the same in the North. On 21 March 1921 Law resigned the leadership, citing exhaustion. He was replaced by Austen Chamberlain. Dissident Conservatives regarded Law as their natural leader, believing that 'if Bonar Law comes again into the arena we have at last got a leader in the Commons ... '.[12] Too weak to capture the party or force an end to the Coalition, dissidents were nonetheless capable of causing turbulence in both by articulating Conservative discontents. If they had captured the party their Conservatism would have had limited electoral appeal. For this reason alone Law would not have endorsed it because, as ever, he was sensitive to threats to party unity and electability.

In Glasgow on 14 February 1922 Law declared his intention of joining no government and defended the Coalition: *I shall certainly be no party to try to bring about a change. I shall do what I can to prevent change until I am satisfied that all events the probabilities are in favour of the change being an improvement in the difficult situation in which the country is placed.*[13]

After the Genoa Conference's failure Law defended the Coalition arguing LG had gone to Genoa confronting complex problems that would not be resolved at one conference, even by LG. Nevertheless, Law cautioned against recognising the USSR, any suggestion of which was guaranteed to inflame Die Hard opinion but that making life as difficult as possible for the Soviet government was counterproductive. Approving of trade with the USSR to reduce unemployment, Law denied trade was *de facto* recognition of the Bolsheviks. The Bolsheviks should only be recognised if they accepted the Tsar's debts, restored property (or paid compensation) and ended propaganda in the Empire and at home.[14]

By early 1921 the accumulated pressure of the war and current problems (for example, unemployment, guerrilla war in Ireland, strikes, and what would today be called 'sleaze') were taking their toll on Law. In his Rectoral Address on 11 March 1921 at Glasgow Law was clearly unwell. His voice was weak and he lost concentration, standing in silence for two minutes: two days later he collapsed after a characteristically vigorous tennis game. Diagnosed as exhausted, his high temperature and blood pressure indicated pneumonia and his doctors decreed six months total rest. On 17 March he resigned all his posts except that of MP. His departure was a major blow to the party and Coalition; 'His debating power, his conciliatory attitude, his candour and disinterestedness, all combined to make him an invaluable asset at any time, most particularly during these years of danger. Moreover he exercised great influence on the Prime Minister, and was a useful link between the two wings of the Coalition.'[15] On 19 March Law left for the South of France to convalesce.

Out of government Law remained a brooding presence. Law had asked Jones to keep him informed about developments in Downing Street and Ireland. Fighting between pro- and anti-treaty forces began in April and jeopardised the settlement. The Dublin government, Law believed, had to act firmly to restore order otherwise the British should do so. Speaking after the funeral of Field Marshal Sir Henry Wilson who had been assassinated on 22 June on the doorstep of his London house, Law had expressed great concern. Recalling his vote for the Treaty, he said *I confess, had I foreseen exactly what the position would have been today. I doubt whether I should have voted for the Treaty.*[16] On 28 June anti-treaty forces had occupied the Four Courts in Dublin, but the resolute action by the Irish government enabled Law to adopt a more moderate position. He did not believe Sinn Fein would be reconciled to partition and *no settlement can be carried in England* unless Ulster was guaranteed self-determination. Law believed only LG was capable of bringing off a settlement and *success would be almost as big as winning the war.* Law was clearly anxious to close down the Irish problem *now that the Unionists in the South are all for agreement with Sinn Fein, I would give the South anything or almost anything, but I would not attempt to force anything on Ulster.*[17] LG 'worried about Bonar, whom he wants to get on his side' and suspected Law was agitating Ulster 'whose resistance appears to be hardening ... Bonar Law still appears to be trying to collect forces to back him in Die Hard attitude.'[18] Law recognised there had to be a settlement as Ireland could not be coerced nor British rule maintained. Many Unionists saw the settlement as rewarding terrorists and a major blow to the Empire's integrity. Rumours circulated that Law was preparing to condemn the settlement but he kept a low profile. On 6 December the agreement with Sinn Fein was signed.

Law made it crystal-clear he supported LG. The only circumstance that would have changed his mind was if Ulster had been denied self-determination. The boundary question remained explosive and he cautioned Ulster against crying 'betrayal', which would complicate relations with Dublin and mainland opinion. Denying the Treaty was *a surrender to murder*, Law was still no enthusiast for the Treaty and doubted any of the signatories were wholly satisfied, *but I ask myself this: What is the alternative? Are we to go back to the conditions of things which prevailed for the past year or two? Nobody would like that*. The settlement should be given a fair chance.[19]

The Coalition was under massive pressure long before the Carlton Club meeting but it was obvious that Law's attitude would be pivotal. With Ulster out of the way foreign policy became Law's main concern. Turkey's defeat of the Greeks in Asia Minor seemed likely to result in the Turks crossing the Dardanelles into the former Ottoman territories transferred to Greece under the Treaty of Sèvres. British troops at Chanak were ordered to stop the Turks. War between Britain and Turkey was avoided by an agreement between local commanders on 11 October but the Chanak Crisis was seen as confirming the Prime Minister's adventurism.

Though horrified, Law resisted efforts to persuade him to challenge the Coalition. He did the next best thing, he wrote to *The Times*. Law agreed the government had been correct to try and stop the Turks advancing into Thrace given the slaughter that followed the Turkish capture of Smyrna in September. However, *the prevention of war and massacre in Constantinople and the Balkans is not specially a British interest. It is in the interest of humanity.* As there was no mechanism for humanitarian intervention the League of Nations were powerless, and as neither the USA, France, Italy, or the Empire were ready to support LG, Law was, in effect, calling for non-intervention and the negotiation of a fair settlement with Turkey. Law then enunciated the basic principle of inter-war foreign policy: *The course of action for our Government seems to me clear. We cannot alone act as the policeman of the world. The financial and social condition of this country makes that impossible.* If the signatories to the Treaty of Sèvres ignored their obligations, Law argued, then *we shall not be able to bear the burden alone, but shall have no alternative except to imitate the Government of the United States and restrict our attention to the safeguarding of the more immediate interests of the Empire.*[20]

Law claimed his letter was intended to help the Coalition but as he knew would happen, it was universally interpreted as a criticism. On 10 October the Cabinet decided to call a general election, a decision that precipitated the crisis. The National Union was scheduled to meet on 15 November and Law believed it would pronounce against the Coalition thus saving him from acting. To any one soliciting his support against the Coalition Law reiterated that his concerns were party unity and his own health. He would not lead a rebellion. By 16 October and the revolt of the Unionist junior ministers it was apparent the party was teetering on the brink.[21] Amery found Law 'very pessimistic about the Party, convinced that nothing would avert a break up and fearing a long exclusion from office, something like the fate of the Party after the break between Peel and Disraeli.' Bridgeman, a rebel, believed that 'If Bonar Law agrees to lead a Unionist Party who will run independently at the next election, I think he would get ¾ of the party at least with him & of course Austen & Co. would have to go.'[22] Law's last hope was his doctor, Sir Thomas Horder. After seeing Horder Law was depressed. Assuming Horder had advised against a return to politics, Davidson was told by Aunt May that

The course of action for our Government seems to me clear. We cannot alone act as the policeman of the world. The financial and social condition of this country makes that impossible.

BONAR LAW

Horder 'had said that Bonar could resume work and that it was *this* that had so depressed Bonar'.[23] This was the break-through; the task was now to convince Law where his duty lay. If he refused his patriotic duty he would betray his party and country, leaving them at the mercy of corrupt liars. Those who placed Law under such pressure knew, or suspected, that his return to politics would kill him. Law and his family knew this too but he could not withstand their use of his own ethic against him.

On the evening of 18 October when Chamberlain visited Law, Law told him that *if* he went to the meeting he would speak against the Coalition. By 8.00 p.m. Law had decided to attend because *there was a higher issue at stake, the unity of his Party*.[24] Law's thought processes cannot of course be reconstructed but the evidence shows him torn between attendance and absence. Within Law two powerful influences were at work: his sense of duty to party and country and the knowledge that following the dictates of the former would kill him. This was tempered by the knowledge that the pre-miership was in his grasp. Many accounts of the Carlton Club meeting focus on Stanley Baldwin's speech. Everyone knew where Baldwin stood on the Coalition, Law's definitive position was unknown and this made his speech far more significant.

Party, Law argued, was the basis of political stability and good governance. Coalition was destabilising because it disrupted the clear line of accountability: *the Party elects a leader, and that the leader chooses the policy, and if the Party does not like the policy they have to get another leader.* Law made no secret of party's centrality to his credo. Even when, as in the war, he relegated party interests, *I did always have at the back of my mind the earnest desire to keep it as a united Party, whatever happened.* Ideally they should hold a referendum on the Coalition but a referendum would split the party. Thus, *in the immediate crisis in front of us I do not personally attach more importance to keeping our Party a united body than to winning the next election.* The only grounds on which Law would agree to Coalition were if there was any prospect of a Labour victory. In fact, Law feared Coalition would help Labour because it would be the only alternative thus attracting all the Coalition's opponents. It would also enervate the Conservative organisation. The Coalition was unstable because half the members of its main element opposed it so even if they voted to remain with LG, the party would split transforming politics. More moderate elements would leave the Coalition Conservative Party and *what is left of the Conservative Party will have become more reactionary ... the reactionary element in our Party has always been there, and must always be there, if it is the sole element, our Party is absolutely lost.*[25] Labour would expand inexorably. There was no compromise position; the choice was between coalition and independence. At the very end of his speech and, he claimed, with reluctance, Law endorsed independence. The Coalition had lost the party's confidence; there was no point in trying to preserve it.

Law's arrival had been accompanied by cheering and 'There were continuous shouts for Bonar and he pulled himself up ... [His speech] evoked tremendous enthusiasm and settled the business.' Crawford commented, 'He looked ill, I thought – his knees more groggy than ever, his face more worn with distress. His voice so weak that people quite close to him had to strain their ears.' Bridgeman concluded that 'If he had not come I think we [anti-Coalitionists] should have won. If he had spoken for Coalition I am pretty sure we should not.'[26] The vote against Coalition was 185 to 88. Law's speech ensured the return to 'normal' politics. Lloyd George resigned immediately, as did Austen Chamberlain. The King sent for

Law who, to the King's astonishment, refused to form a government until his party had formally acknowledged him as leader. A meeting was hurriedly arranged for 23 October at the Hotel Cecil and, acknowledged as the party's leader, Law became Prime Minister. We should not, perhaps, underestimate Law's ambition, after all 'the Premiership had escaped him twice'. Reflecting on these events Davidson recalled, 'Bonar Law was a funny fellow, because in spite of his very quiet, very domesticated and in many ways simple character, he did want to be Prime Minister. But it wasn't the power … it was that he would like people to feel that he was fit for it.'[27]

The Coalition's death created an opportunity to recast Conservative politics around resistance to Socialism. The main obstacle to this had been the Coalition and the threatened Conservative split that would bring Labour to power. The Conservative Party *would be the party which, in the public mind at least, would be supposed to represent class interests, class privileges, and everything which we call re-action. If that happened I can imagine nothing worse, not only for the Party but for the nation.* Law made no policy pronouncements but insisted, as in 1911, on unity and loyalty to his leadership. His government's defining characteristic would be *a difference of temperament*, specified by its ethos not policy: *What this country needs above everything else at the moment is conservatism in the broad sense of the word. What is needed is tranquillity, freedom from adventures and commitments both at home and abroad. The country and the world is left in a very bad position as the result of the War. If it is to recover it will not be by attempts from above, it will be by the work of the people of the country; and*

'If he {Bonar Law} had not come I think we {anti-Coalitionists} should have won. If he had spoken for Coalition I am pretty sure we should not.'

BRIDGEMAN

The 1922 Committee

Andrew Bonar Law's tenure as Prime Minister is too short to have changed the role or the office in any significant way. He might be recalled, however, as the only Prime Minister to have been born abroad, as the first Presbyterian to hold the office, the first businessman, or even as Roy Jenkins has suggested, the first 'ordinary man'. He also holds the unenviable record of being the Prime Minister of the 20th century with the shortest time in office: he served for only 209 days, compared with Anthony Eden's 279 days.

His impact on his party was much greater, managing to hold the Conservatives together by leading them from the right to the centre. He played down his role with the memorable words: *I must follow them, I am their Leader*. One institution of the party is connected with the memory of Andrew Bonar Law to this day: the 1922 Committee, the entire body of backbenchers in the Conservative Party. It is said to take its name from a meeting of Conservative MPs in the Carlton Club on 19 October 1922. At this meeting, the most dramatic intervention had come from the previously little-known Stanley Baldwin, who had recently been promoted to President of the Board of Trade. 'He is a dynamic force', he said of Lloyd George, 'and it is from this very fact that our troubles, in our opinion, arose … It is owing to that dynamic force and that remarkable personality, that the Liberal Party, to which he formerly belonged, has been smashed to pieces; and it is my firm conviction that, in time, the same thing will happen to our own party.' Yet it was Bonar Law's speech, hesitant and fumbling as it was, which swayed the greater number of votes, as he eventually made it clear that he believed that the coalition should come to an end. (Dick Leonard, *A Century of Premiers* (Palgrave Macmillan, London: 2005) p 91.) This sudden taste of power suggested the need for an organisation through which backbenchers might continue to exert influence. The executive of the 1922 Committee meets weekly when the House of Commons is sitting and the chairman, a senior member of the party, has direct access to the leader.

my idea of the real methods of dealing with it is to leave free play to the individual initiative; to avoid attempts at improvement which at another time would be very desirable and very necessary.[28] Not since Lord Salisbury had inaction been placed at the centre of politics. Acclaimed unanimously as leader, Law went to the Palace and then called an election.

The 1922 Conservative manifesto is the most original in British history. Written largely by Amery, its essence was Law's. His government would, he insisted, be clearly distinguished from LG's: *LG was all right as a drummer in a cavalry charge in war but we did not want a drummer in a hospital.*[29] Thus, *The crying need of the nation at this moment – a need which in my judgement far exceeds any other – is that we should have tranquillity and stability at home and abroad so that free scope should be given to initiative and enterprise of our citizens, for it is in that way far more than by any action of the Government that we can hope to recover from the economic and social results of the war.*[30]

The brevity of Law's Premiership means his manifesto and speeches assume great significance, offering an insight into what a full-term Law government might have done. Law would have tried innovative governance: *There are many measures of legislative and administrative importance which, in themselves, would be desirable ... But I do not feel that they can, at this moment, claim precedence over the nation's first need, which is, in every walk of life, to get on with its work with the minimum interference at home and of disturbance abroad.* Whether Law or the country would be permitted this tranquillity is a different question.

In Glasgow on 26 October Law repeated his well-known view that the Treaty of Versailles had been unrealistic in the reparations sought from Germany. He recognised the strength of public opinion, especially in France, and agreed *We need something from Germany if we can get it ... to get everything which*

Germany can reasonably be asked to pay ... [but] *the whole well being of Europe, and therefore the World, depends on common action.* On 3 November Law expressed his desire, after LG's excitements, for equilibrium with Britain *loyally fulfilling the obligations we have undertaken, but resolutely determined not to extend our commitments, and should reasonable occasion arise to curtail them.* The war had been won by co-operation with France and Law was adamant that *our relationship with France is the keynote ... of our foreign policy.* Reparation problems could not be resolved without the USA but America was retreating into isolation. Law's policy was obvious and platitudinous; *The maintenance of our friendship and good understanding with the United States, based not on any formal alliance, but a community of inherited ideals as well as on recent comradeship in arms, must always be a principle aim of British policy.* Whether Presidents Harding and Coolidge's America recognised a 'community of inherited ideals' and 'comradeship in arms' was moot. In the Near East Law would give his Foreign Secretary, Lord Curzon, the freedom to negotiate a settlement with Turkey at Lausanne. He wanted Britain out; *Heaven knows that our responsibilities are great enough ... we don't want to increase them ... one of the things that will rejoice us most must will be ... that our troops can be brought home.* The same criteria applied to Mesopotamia and Palestine that were a financial drain and an ever-present threat of war. On 7 November he declared: *We are being asked to say that we will get out of Mesopotamia and Palestine. I wish we had never gone there.*

Law's accession to the premiership meant a protectionist was at last in Number 10. This, and post-war turbulence and unemployment, encouraged tariff reformers to believe their hour had come. In 1917 Law had expressed the view that free trade's dominance was over. Whilst nothing could be done yet, *I can say for myself and I think all my colleagues would say that we would not be members of any Government which did not make a change in our fiscal policy.*[31] The 1918 compromise produced the Safeguarding of Industries Act (1921) and Law would not go beyond this. There was no mention of tariff reform in the manifesto, which reflected Law's desire for tranquillity and avoiding any issue that might jeopardise victory. Convinced *he would be weak in the Commons*, Law felt vulnerable on tariff reform. *If I do not safeguard myself now*, he told Tom Jones, *by some pronouncement and reserve the right to impose certain tariffs for the sake of revenue and keep down taxation I shall have to have another election to do so because it would be said I had no mandate.*[32] Tariff reformers were content Law was PM and that the door remained open. The manifesto spoke warmly, if vaguely, of the need to develop Empire trade and Law promised a conference of Dominions. Subject to their approval, the aim was to promote mutually beneficial co-operation. In Glasgow on 26 October Law emphasised; *I am not thinking of fiscal measures ... What I said about leaving things alone applies here also.* On 7 November he opined *any violent change would be bad at the present time* and so *this Parliament will not make any fundamental change in the fiscal system of this country.* On Ireland, the manifesto and his speeches repeated Law's view that the treaty should be made to work.

The manifesto recognised unemployment as the government's chief concern and committed Law's government to sensible emergency relief measures. However, *the first essential is to reduce expenditure to the lowest attainable level in the hope that the taxpayer may find some relief from the burden of taxation which not only presses so heavily upon individuals, but is the greatest clog upon the wheels of national industry.* Though economically orthodox he was under no illusion that cutting spending would be easy. So, *I am not going to make any wild promises; but I also know that if it can be done, it must be done. Without it there* is no possibility of relieving the burden of taxation. Law's commitment to the £500-a-year man was clear. Deflation threatened confrontation with organised labour. On 7 November Law rejected the charge that a Conservative government would attack the unions' political funds, reducing their ability to engage in politics. No one, Law believed, should be compelled to pay the political levy: *But we are going to have no rash action about it. Before we dreamt of dealing with it we should consult both trade union leaders and the employers; and if we have to do anything, we should certainly try to get an arrangement that seemed fair to reasonable members of trade unions.* Making it more difficult to elect Labour MPs would be *a national misfortune* because *it is a good education for the Labour members and it is a good thing for the nation that a movement of that kind should be constitutional, and be in the House of Commons and not underground.*

Law distinguished between the Labour Party and labour. In Leeds on 14 November he identified himself with the Disraelian tradition. To his opponents' charge that the Conservative Party was the party of dukes and millionaires, Law retorted, *we are not such fools. You know the size of the franchise. You know there is not one of my colleagues in the last House of Commons, and there will not be one in the next, who could have his seat there unless he had the support of the millionaires and dukes, or even the middle classes, but the support of the mass of the people of the country.* The Conservatives' object was a prosperous working class in harmony with other classes and the national interest. Bolshevism was a terrible warning: *Socialism and all the rest is the millennium, you can only get the millennium by passing through the horrors which have devastated Russia.*

In the election the Conservatives polled 5.5 million votes, 345 of its 438 candidates were elected and the party won 38.2 per cent of the votes cast and 56 per cent of seats on a turnout of 71.3 per cent. The Conservative Party did not markedly improve on its 1918 position. It was strengthened by the departure of the Southern Irish MPs, the collapse of the Lloyd George Liberals (from 133 to 62), and the surge in Labour's vote from 2.3 million votes and 63 seats in 1918 to 4.2 million votes and 142 seats. Despite the election of minority governments in 1923 and 1929 the modern party system was created in 1922 and 'The Bonar Law government heralded in the clearest possible terms the return of political normality, founded on orthodox party machines and rivalries.'[33] Law's victory was very much a personal one and was infused with his political personality. It reflected Law's gloom but also that of much of the nation. Mass Conservatism could not be built on hostility to Sinn Fein, anti-Bolshevism, deflation and the moans of the £500-a-year man but required an ideological mobilisation against the industrial working class. This could, and did, appeal beyond the middle class as the organised working class could be portrayed as a moral, political and economic threat to the *status quo*. Anti-collectivist and morally censorious, this proved to be an enduring appeal.[34] Law's emerging grand coalition was unstable. Its heterogeneity – the £500-a-year man, women, the City, manufacturing, small businessmen, the non-unionised working class, the property owner – meant a continuous balancing and re-balancing by concession to various groups. 'Die Hard-ism' was too narrow electorally and to ideologically negative to form the basis of a successful Conservative statecraft in the new democracy.

Attacked for negativity, Law rounded on his critics. In Glasgow on 26 October, for example, he declared, *You will say that it is purely negative. It is intended to be ... I think we must have as little legislation as possible, that we must leave things alone more or less where we can.* In the Glasgow speech Law distinguished stability from stagnation: *I want tranquillity and stability ...*

but that does not mean I am satisfied with the world … There are times when it is good to sit still and go slowly. Others felt his message was mundane: 'There is something drab and uninspiring about B Law's appeal to our commercial instincts, and though he boasts of being the plain man, our position in the world cannot quite be judged on the principles of a chartered accountant.'[35] Law's colleagues were derided as 'the second XI', possessing 'second class brains' a judgement, which, not surprisingly, he rejected forcefully. *We may not*, he told the National Union in December, *have … a monopoly of first-class brains, but we are, I hope, and I believe, a Government composed of men with good judgement – and what is perhaps not less important, we are a government of first-class loyalty.*[36]

LG believed that if Law had a majority the result would be five years of reaction. Law reiterated the commitment made in 1911 when first elected leader; he would not be a member of a reactionary party or lead a reactionary government. His demeanour suggested otherwise. During the election Jones recalled 'a long exposition of the virtues of individualism and the motives which moved mankind on the usual lines proper to a Glasgow business man. I begged him to shew some real sympathy with Glasgow unemployed, described the groups of half starved men I had seen at the street corners when there in June and how I had been told that the birds were nesting in the cranes on the banks of the Clyde.'[37] There was a perception, which grew stronger in government, that personally and politically Law's politics and strategy were an evolutionary blind alley.

Part Two

THE LEADERSHIP

Chapter 7: Prime Minister

At the Carlton Club Law had made clear his conviction that his early retirement was more likely than not but there is no evidence he intended to retire when he did. Close observers sensed he might last six months but acknowledged that Law's dolefulness could disguise a determination to carry on. His doctors advised there was no reason to suppose he could not bear the burdens of office but Law doubted he could do so for long and if he believed himself incapable he would resign.[1] As he told his constituency chair, *My decision to resign was in the end a sudden one*. Even so, Law's government has a distinctly provisional air due partly to his determination that his government should do as little as possible but also because the issues dominating his premiership – reparations and debt, the Near East, unemployment – were not amenable to speedy resolution.

Parliament convened on 20 November for a brief three-week session to deal with the constitutional provisions of the Irish treaty. Law never believed the treaty *per se* would resolve the Irish problem but Ulster had been secured. The manifesto rammed home the position that the Treaty was the only viable policy and had to be approved by 6 December. If it were not, the result would be calamitous. The Dublin parliament and the British electorate had approved it; there was no alternative.[2] The Treaty was duly approved on 6 December.

With Ireland disposed of, foreign policy filled the vacuum.

In early November Hankey, the Cabinet Secretary, warned Law that abandoning Chanak might result in disaster: 'He made light of it. I can see that their real hope is that, if as usual the French and Italians refuse to assist us in offering force to the Turks we shall be able to withdraw "honourably" on the ground that we cannot do the job alone. A nice position when the British Empire cannot stand up to Turkey?'[3]

Soon after becoming Prime Minister he stated, *we must have regard to our condition … We have suffered as much as anyone … we cannot be the Don Quixotes of the world. We want to help the world, but we cannot, and … we will not do it alone.*[4] Central to Law's foreign policy was a perception of economic weakness and imperial over-stretch requiring extensive budget cuts and the shedding of commitments to focus on Britain's vital interests.

True to his word Law left Curzon alone after he left for Lausanne on 17 November and he said nothing publicly. The talks lasted from 20 November to 4 February, ending when the Turks refused to sign. Government equivocation was reflected in Law's gnomic statement: *There is war weariness in this country. Everyone here desires, above everything else, to avoid the risk of war, but, if it inevitable, it will have to take place. I sincerely trust that it will not, for I do not believe that there is danger of it.*[5] Particularly problematic was the Kurdish territory of Mosul that contained massive oil deposits and which was now part of the British client state of Iraq. Curzon feared Law might surrender Mosul to appease the Turks while Law feared Curzon might involve him in a war over oil. Despite prodding from the Cabinet Curzon refused to be deflected and, ultimately, Mosul remained in Iraq. Speaking on a Liberal amendment to the King's Speech seeking a drastic cut in the British presence in Iraq, Law agreed with the sentiment. His government was not responsible for Britain's presence and he would rather not be there. However, Britain had treaty commitments to Iraq (*which we have set up*) and a moral obligation to the Iraqis but this was not an open-ended commitment. Britain would not withdraw unilaterally and *we do not want to stop ... for any oil that is in Mesopotamia.*[6]

The uncertain basis of Law's foreign policy was France. Law feared that foreign policy could destroy his government but Britain lacked reliable partners: *It is true that I attach the utmost importance to maintaining a good understanding with France. I may have to choose between two evils – between a breach with France, which would mean chaos in Europe, or concessions which would also involve great mischief ...*[7] German reparations, however, threatened Anglo-French relations. Early in 1921 the French had won a ruling that Germany was defaulting on its reparations payments and Poincaré, the French Prime Minister, made no secret of his intention to occupy the Ruhr unless payment resumed. Law was convinced the reparation clauses were unworkable but with France as the centrepiece of his foreign policy, he could do little. Law was deeply pessimistic about finding a solution and feared serious, possible fatal, consequences for the Weimar Republic and Europe.

On 9 December Poincaré, Theunis (the Belgian PM) and Mussolini (the recently-installed Italian PM whom Law thought a lunatic) met in London to seek a solution. Many in the foreign policy establishment feared Law would be out of his depth. He bought time, persuading Poincaré to meet again in Paris in the New Year. Hankey approved of Law employing many of LG's wiles, noting admiringly, 'Bonar Law is more tricky than I suspected.'[8] Nevertheless, Law was convinced the French would invade. Law went to Paris on 2 January with proposals for a moratorium as a prelude to a general settlement. In Paris there was a full and frank exchange of views. Law regarded Poincaré's policy as contradictory and self-defeating ('trying to cut beef steaks from the cow which they would like to milk'), making it crystal clear 'that the British were prepared to support nothing which ... would help to produce disaster in Germany and rob the British tax-payer ... '[9] Poincaré, whom Law disliked, refused to compromise. On 11 January French and Belgian troops occupied the Ruhr, and Law had no option other than to acquiesce. Responding to calls to 'do something', Law warned action beyond speeches (which the French ignored) meant that *We would have to prepare ourselves for the possibility of enforcing our will upon France by war.* France, he reminded the House, was totally convinced of its case, so for the moment there was no alternative to allowing events to run their course.[10]

Law's approach to France and the Ruhr was intimately related his concern about the health of the political economy and that taxpayers were exhausted. Reparations, he felt, had destroyed the German middle class with calamitous political consequences for Weimar, so realism was in everyone's – debtors' and creditors' – interests. This applied to Britain's war debts. Law would neither destroy the middle class by taxation nor impoverish the country for the United States. Law condemned as folly paying of a fixed amount of debt over a fixed period; repayment should be conditional on the health of the domestic and international economy.[11]

'Bonar Law is more tricky than I suspected.'

HANKEY

The shift of power in the global economy posed the question: what was to be Britain's relationship with the USA? Law's focus on financial strength was a tacit recognition of the country's vulnerability, which led to a focus on the Empire (symbolised by sanctioning the Singapore naval base) and European stability. Britain needed US co-operation in areas where British and American interests intersected (reflected in the 1921 Washington Naval Treaty) but there was little evidence of American willingness to engage. Britain's debt to the USA, largely for supplies purchased for France and Italy, were more than balanced by their debt to Britain. The British never denied the legal obligation to pay the debt but that it was more sensible to negotiate a general settlement. Policy was based on the Balfour Note (August 1922) whereby Britain undertook to recover sufficient debt from France and Italy to repay the UK's to the USA. However, the US was demanding payment in full and French repayments depended on German reparation.[12] In early January 1923 Baldwin, the Chancellor of the Exchequer, and Montague Norman, the Governor of the Bank of England, sailed for New York to negotiate a settlement.

Baldwin had the power to negotiate but not to sign an agreement. Law favoured delay; Baldwin a speedy settlement which he and Norman believed necessary to reduce America's isolationism and avoid undermining Britain's credibility by seemingly welshing on its debts. Cutting a long story short, the US offered repayment at 3 per cent for 10 years and 3.5 per cent for 52 years with a 1 per cent sinking fund that entailed repayments of £34 million (10 years) and £40 million (52 years). Law wanted to offer 2.5 per cent. The Cabinet, unanimously opposed to the offer, agreed with Law that the interest rate was 'intolerably unjust' and, for some reason, believed American public opinion would reject it. Baldwin was told the US offer was unreasonable and the delegation was recalled. Excessive repayment, Law believed, would reduce the country's standard of living for a generation, that the Americans were guilty of usury and that they were seeking to weaken their main competitor. Baldwin left the US convinced this was the best offer and the Debt Commission warned him

American Debt Settlement

The most notable event in Stanley Baldwin's brief Chancellorship was his handling of the American debt settlement. The British position, firmly held by Bonar Law and most of his Cabinet, was that all inter-Allied debts should be cancelled, but that in any event Britain should not be required to repay its debts to America until comparable arrangements were in place for the repayment of its own loans to its European allies, notably France and Italy, and the achievement of a realistic deal on German reparations. On 27 December 1922 Baldwin left for Washington, accompanied by Montague Norman, the Governor of the Bank of England, with a firm mandate not to agree a settlement involving payments in excess of £25 million a year. They encountered a new, the first post-war American administration headed by President Warren Harding, which was more 'America first' than that of the internationalist Wilson. Because federal expenditures had soared during the war, greatly increasing the national debt, Andrew Mellon, installed as secretary of the treasury, insisted on government frugality; no unnecessary federal expense would be countenanced. If that involved a less than generous response to Britain's requests, this seemed a small price to pay for the restoration of the 'normalcy' the president had promised. The Republican-dominated US Congress demanded cash on the nail. The best that Baldwin could achieve under the circumstances was a funding agreement providing for annual payments of £34 million for the first ten years, increasing to £40 million for the remaining 52 years of the agreement. Upon his return from the US, Baldwin recommended acceptance on the grounds that this was the best settlement obtainable. When the Cabinet met, Bonar Law made it clear that he would resign if the terms were accepted, but only one of his colleagues supported his view. The meeting was hastily adjourned overnight, and on the following morning a letter, over the pseudonym 'Colonial', appeared in *The Times*, setting out the same arguments that Bonar Law had used in the Cabinet meeting – it subsequently emerged that Law himself had written the letter.

acceptance was the key to Anglo-American co-operation. On 14 January Baldwin warned Law of the strong pressures in the US and urged acceptance but Law made it clear that he remained strongly opposed, although he postponed a Cabinet decision until Baldwin returned. Attendance was thin and several of those present seemed concerned about Law's hard-line but deferred to him. Law had discussed the offer with Reginald McKenna to gauge City opinion, which opposed acceptance.[13]

Docking at Southampton, Baldwin was confronted by a press gaggle fired up by reports in the US press and, believing he was off the record, blurted out his opinion that the offer was the best available. In Cabinet on 30 January Baldwin repeated this. Law was appalled and 'in his firm and gentle way [stated] that whatever we thought, he was determined not to agree to the American proposal and would resign rather than do so'.[14] Resignation was, of course, Law's favourite strategy when backed into a corner. His reaction certainly caused consternation but this time the Cabinet's response differed. Law had made little effort to prepare the Cabinet, although it was well aware of his attitude, some ministers resented his attempt to bounce the Cabinet. Only two ministers supported Law, Amery noting waspishly that both were Scots, and to forestall a crisis the Cabinet adjourned. One Cabinet member was 'astonished' by the vigour of Law's opposition and that this implied 'it would be better for us to default as the French are doing to us'.[15] In an effort to whip up a groundswell of opposition Law wrote anonymously to *The Times*. Isolated and with his health causing concern, he had failed to persuade his colleagues or impose his will. He had used his most powerful weapon to no effect. Law believed the Cabinet's decision was disastrous but it would be equally disastrous for the government to lose its Prime Minister.

By now the City had changed its mind. On 30 January, with Law's knowledge, a group of senior ministers met in the Lord Chancellor's room and agreed to implore Law not to resign. He agreed. A specially convened (and brief) Cabinet accepted Baldwin's proposals. 'Bonar,' Amery noted, 'is certainly apt to be rather autocratic in his methods but realises that he could hardly force the whole Cabinet to do what they felt to be a great mistake simply to comply with his wishes.' Hankey believed the government had come close to breaking up but 'In the end ... Bonar Law "piped down" owing to the extreme difficulties in which his party would be placed if he resigned.'[16] The Carlton Club and the US debt episodes demonstrate once again that party loyalty was the key to Law's political personality. Defeat depressed Law, the effect relieved only by the birth of his first grandchild and from this point Law's interest in the premiership waned.

The parliamentary session began in mid-February. The King's Speech was compared to 'Bonar's customary ginger ale, rather dry and uninspiring but will serve its purpose.'[17] In the election Law's former Chief Whip had expressed surprise at his ability to win over voters. 'The electors,' he wrote, 'are rather taken by his claim to be one of themselves – a simple honest fellow, without brilliance or rhetoric, but equally without stunts and blunders and tergiversations.' The canny ex-whip doubted 'this rather vapid ideal of Tranquillity' would survive contact with political reality and doubted it had the legs to evolve into a governing strategy.[18] By March Law, his government and his strategy appeared exhausted. 'I have never,' Jones confessed in his diary, 'seen him so depressed. I never saw L.G. even at the blackest time of the war in such a gloomy frame of mind.' Cabinet members were expressing disquiet at 'negativity'.

Amery and Neville Chamberlain, for example, discussed 'the need for looking ahead and having some policy on Social Reform. We also agreed that, in order to break the new habit of treating the Cabinet like a business committee and hurrying through a few items on the agenda ... we should take the opportunity to ask occasional questions on the state of foreign and other general matters in order to start discussion'.[19]

In February the government's majority fell to 22 on a motion calling for universal old age pensions and in April it was defeated by five votes in a snap division on unemployment amongst ex-servicemen. Also in April Austen Chamberlain rebuffed Law's offer of office. On 3 March the government lost two seats (Mitcham and Willesden East) to the Labour and Liberal parties respectively, and on 6 March Labour captured Liverpool Edge Hill.

On 29 March Parliament rose and Law left for Torquay to rest. Parliament reassembled on 10 April and although Law's throat seemed a little better, he was unable to answer questions or speak in debates. Baldwin took over these responsibilities. Law continued to chair Cabinet, albeit with difficulty, and his government recovered its equilibrium. There was no major fall-out from the by-election losses and Baldwin's budget on 16 April projected a balanced budget and some taxes were cut. The government's crisis seemed to have passed. Ministers were finding their feet and growing in confidence but the major question remained: how long could Law continue as Prime Minister? Cabinets were even more perfunctory, press speculation was unabated, and at the Duke of York's wedding on 26 April Law looked frail, grey and gaunt.

For months Law had problems speaking and seemed tired. A common judgement was that defeat over the American debt had completed his disillusion and drained whatever zest he had for the Premiership. When Parliament rose in April an exhausted Law was instructed to take a month's break, opting for a cruise to Genoa he hinted that if he felt no better he would reconsider his position. Despite some press optimism his decline continued and Rudyard Kipling, whom Law joined at Aix-les-Bains when he left the cruise prematurely, was so shocked by his decline he cabled for Beaverbrook. When Beaverbrook arrived Law was in pain. Heavily sedated, he was not surprisingly depressed. Taking charge, Beaverbrook despatched Law and his party to Paris where on 17 May Sir Thomas Horder examined Law. Law had inoperable throat cancer. In constant pain, able to speak only in a loud whisper, and subject to sedation, Law concluded he had reached the state of affairs he had identified in November. On 19 May he returned to London. Too ill to attend an audience with the King, Law tendered his resignation in writing. Controversy dogged Law's final hours in office. Who should succeed him? Curzon or Baldwin? Vast quantities of ink have been spilt on the succession because of Law's reluctance to name his successor. Even if it is the case that the Davidson Memorandum, urging Baldwin over Curzon, did not reflect Law's true opinions this hardly matters as Law did not express them. The point is that Curzon was widely believed to be unsuitable – personally and politically – in the new democracy. Baldwin became Prime Minister.

Law did not resign from the House but took no further part in politics. Refusing all honours, he spent his time at Brighton undergoing palliative care, and briefly at Le Touquet where he even managed a round of golf. By September his condition was worsening rapidly and he returned to his London home at Onslow Gardens where, nursed by his daughter Ishbel and watched over by Beaverbrook, he died on 30 October 1923. His express wish to be buried next to his wife in Helensburgh cemetery was ignored and he was interred in Westminster Abbey on 5 November.

Part Three

THE LEGACY

Chapter 8: Assessment

In December 1999 a poll of 20 prominent academics, politicians and commentators conducted for BBC Radio 4's *The Westminster Hour*, ranked Law 13th out of 19 PMs. In 2000 the British Politics Group, a network of British and American academics, on the basis of 20 responses ranked Law 18th out of 19. In *The Times* (27 December 1999) the late Lord Jenkins of Hillhead, himself no stranger to political failure, bracketed Law with Eden and Major as failures. The most extensive rating of Prime Ministers, using poll data and expert evaluations, placed Law as 16th out of 20; political scientists ranked him 18th, historians put him 16th.[1] Law's ranking owes much to academic focus on fame, popularity and longevity as the basis of reputation, which, in turn, influences evaluation. Law's 'Don't Knows' were the third highest, co-equal with Campbell-Bannerman. Jenkins argued that to have a major impact a prime minister needed at least five years of office and the evidence suggests a correlation between tenure and ranking.

Lloyd George thought Law was a good chairman but no leader, 'He is always waiting for a course, which was inevitable. He could not speak to the country. His words do not travel. He had not the gift of wireless speech. He has always rested on a more energetic personality.' Few politicians, including LG, used radio effectively (the first was Baldwin) and in Law's case, a lack of energy signified neither ineffectiveness nor subordination. One judgement was that Law 'lacked the resilience of Lloyd George, the enthusiasm of Gladstone, the aloofness of [Balfour], the cynicism of Campbell-Bannerman, or the festiveness of Asquith – all qualities and temperaments which enabled the great people to shake of their anxieties.'[2] This is wrong. Law had always approach decisions cautiously to avoid precipitate action and his caution was often misinterpreted as anxiety or doubt, moreover at this time he was ill, sensing perhaps his death.

Having been *de facto* Deputy Prime Minister and a close observer of Asquith and LG, Law came to Number 10 with clear ideas of what it was to be PM: *The Prime Minister if he is to do his work has to be something more than one of a number of Cabinet colleagues. He has to be the leader of the Government and the leader of the nation, and to do that he must have the support of those who are working for him.* He believed the Cabinet's task was *to strengthen the Prime Minister and not to thwart him by endless opposition.*[3] Law favoured the speedy despatch of business, which civil servants approved and Cabinet windbags disliked. Never a commanding presence in Cabinet ('You could barely hear him at the Cabinet a yard off'), he nevertheless 'misled many people into the belief that he was weak because his manner and voice were so gentle, and his heart so kind'.[4] Those who sat in both LG's and Law's cabinet were struck forcibly by the difference in style. Amery, for example, recorded:

'Bonar firmly discourages full dress debates and as regards the India question would not have it discussed at all but promptly remitted it to a small committee. (19 December 1922).

The Prime Minister if he is to do his work has to be something more than one of a number of Cabinet colleagues. He has to be the leader of the Government and the leader of the nation.

BONAR LAW

There is very little talk and things are likely cut and dried. In fact with all his mildness of demeanour Bonar is really much more of an autocrat than LG (15 January 1923).

His general attitude towards most things is negative and I have taken in Cabinet to counting how often he begins a sentence with "I am afraid" or "I fear". (23 February).

We then got thought the agenda in 25 minutes and then did a little talking at large on the Eastern situation, and the Ruhr. (14 March).'

Law had often procrastinated, which makes his intransigence over the debt settlement puzzling, but equally, there were occasions when Law suddenly blazed up and dug in his heels usually over an issue that he felt deeply. Ulster was one, so was debt. Whilst this might be an advantage in Opposition it was dangerous in government and the debt episode was antithetical to Law's conception of the proper PM–Cabinet relationship. Whereas intransigence over Ulster cemented Law's authority, intransigence over debt weakened it.

Law's style reflected both the election's tranquillity theme and his conviction that government should less active than LG's. Law, for example, endorsed enthusiastically the Ministry of Labour's policy of non-intervention that developed as a reaction to the previous 14 years. Spectacular industrial unrest before 1914, the war, the Ministry of Munitions and LG encouraged intervention but government should intervene, Law believed, only if essential services were threatened. Workers and employers should settle their differences but 'Nothing is easier than to intervene, few things are more difficult than to refrain from interfering.'[5] This underlay Law's refusal to see a deputation of unemployed marchers. Law insisted that *the work must be left to the Departmental heads ... the Prime Minister could not do it all himself ... '*. Ministers *were not servants of the Prime Minister* [and] *it is essential that people outside should be made to realise that it is under the ordinary method of government that the work has to be done ...*[6]

When a deputation of the unemployed were seeking an interview with Law, Downing Street requested police files on the leaders and *The Daily Herald* was, inadvertently, excluded from briefings which, when combined with the new approach, made Law and his government seem harsh and unsympathetic. Law's refusal to see the deputation provoked a furious response from Labour MPs. In a period of domestic political and economic crisis the instant recourse to the Prime Minister, Law believed, subverted good government. *If they got it into their heads that they can achieve any object ... by coming to London, it will not be the only deputation to march to London, and you will find that in hundreds of cases the same plan is tried again.*[7] LG's tendency to leap in was self-defeating; encouraging further pressure, and risking overload whereas Law was seeking to ease pressure by reducing expectations.

Law told a TUC delegation he could not see why Parliament remaining in session or him receiving deputations would ease unemployment. He would not borrow: unemployment would be reduced by a balanced budget and reduced taxation; industry had to make profits and his government's task was to create conditions conducive to profit making. *We are*, Law told the TUC, *doing what we can to get employment, and we are doing all we can to restore sound finance* and, *before these bodies began to march to London – and I think we can imagine nothing more foolish than that they should waste whatever money they had and their shoe leather ... merely to make a demonstration* [which was] *propaganda against the present Conservative Government ... you cannot expect us to assist it.*[8]

Law's conception of the government's role in the economy was minimalist. Law willingly conceded, for example, that conditions in the mining districts were *horribly bad* but *does not your proposal*, he asked a mineworkers' deputation, *come down to this, that government must in some way subsidise the trade?* Given current conditions *I could see no remedy* and mineworkers should wait for his government's policy to work. *What*, he asked rhetorically, *can Government do? It is easy to say* [it] *is the business of Government to put right. How exactly can they put it right?*[9] He complained frequently that those who sought his and the government's intervention believed that *I was not merely a dictator but actually all-powerful, and could do anything that was asked. That is not so.*[10]

What can Government do? It is easy to say {it} is the business of Government to put right. How exactly can they put it right?

BONAR LAW

Law's preference was always for market forces and the private sector. In December he told the Mineworkers' Federation of Great Britain in no uncertain terms that he was powerless. *I quite see your case – You are working hard and not getting any reward and you are hoping that the Government is hoping to give it to you. I cannot.* Law warned businessmen: *We have in the House of Commons … an element such as we have never seen before because there were enough* [Labour MPs] *to create a serious opposition, so that extent, our whole industrial system is challenged.* He urged railway directors to place orders and create work without, of course, damaging shareholder interests, and government would do all it could safeguard investment and profits.[11] To a second delegation of mineworkers Law refused an inquiry into the industry and recommended they put their faith not in government but the laws of supply and demand. Coal prices had rocketed as a result of the Ruhr occupation, *There is, as you know, a boom in your trade* [high prices] *will be reflected later in your wages … .* Difficulties in the building trade flowed, he believed, from competition between the public and private builders and *I would rather try some scheme that would get in into the hands of private enterprise.* He disputed the contention *that every person in need is entitled to look to the State for either work or maintenance.*[12]

This reconfiguration of the state's relationship with producer groups was not entirely Law's doing. Law and the political-bureaucratic élites were determined to retreat from LG's corporatism to reduce the pressure on the central state, reduce expectations, and thereby promote governability. Government was inevitably more responsive to business interests and endorsed orthodox economics but organised labour was not actively excluded – either politically or electorally. Having observed LG closely Law was ambivalent about his approach to the premiership. Law clearly admired LG's great energy, which he readily conceded he lacked but which was inappropriate for the country. Law allowed ministers to get on with their jobs under his (and the Cabinet's) general guidance, an approach that worked well with Curzon but which was less successful with Baldwin. This was a clear rejection of LG's 'presidential' style but was equally a rejection of Asquith's indolence. The result was a significant stage in the evolution in the evolution of the Premiership.

Hankey was apprehensive about Law's re-emergence, believing it boded ill for the Cabinet Secretariat. Part of Law's suspicion stemmed from doubts about Hankey's close association with LG and his ability to serve him loyally. Hankey reassured Law who nevertheless remained convinced the bureaucracy must be reduced. On 26 October Law appeared to commit his government to abolition. *We must have an agenda at our meetings, and we must have a definite record of decisions*, Law stated, *But there is no need for the big body that was necessary during the War and immediately after it …* What was left of the secretariat would be located in the Treasury, the central department.[13] Law told Tom Jones that,

When I joined the first Cabinet of which I was a member I remember saying to the Prime Minister, 'This is awful. There is no agenda.' I had never seen any business conducted in this way. His reply was, 'Every new member of a Cabinet says the same thing; but he got used to it.' We have no right to get used to it. We must have an agenda at our meetings, and we must have a definite record of decisions. In the old days nothing was taken down Members and the Cabinet get away with different views as to what the decision was. That was fatal.[14]

This sparked an epic Whitehall turf war between Hankey and Warren Fisher at the Treasury and led to Law's single innovation in governance. After offering budget and staff cuts, and transferring functions to the Foreign Office, Hankey asked Law 'if he intended to have a Cabinet Secretariat or to scrap it. He at once replied he intended to continue the system of Cabinet conclusions, which he thought essential to businesslike procedure'.[15] The Glasgow speech seemed to renege on this and Hankey came close to resignation after *The Times* on 27 October equated the secretariat with a Prime Minister's department that was 'in subversion of well tried constitutional practices and safeguards'. Law returned to the question of the secretariat on 2 November. His main motivation was not so much cost but concern about the quality and tone of government as part of his wider tranquillity theme. This was reaction to LG's premiership and the centralisation of power in Number 10 and the consequent reduction in the Cabinet's influence.[16] Critics were confusing two institutions. The Cabinet Secretariat, created in 1916, had emerged from the Committee on Imperial Defence (formed in 1909), that took minutes, circulated papers, recorded decisions and provided a central co-ordinating function in the core executive. This was a major innovation and despite its name was a significant augmentation of prime ministerial power. The Prime Minister's

Secretariat, known as 'The Garden Suburb', had been created by LG as his personal policy staff and to engage in various political black arts. The Garden Suburb quickly developed an unsavoury and sinister reputation as an extension of LG's mercurial and unprincipled political persona. Though largely exaggerated this cemented its reputation as unconstitutional and it symbolised the dangers of LG's system.[17]

The Secretariat's political prominence in 1922 testifies to the importance Law attached to tranquillity and stability. LG's bloated machine reflected a governance that neither the country nor Law wanted, so the Garden Suburb was abolished but the Secretariat retained. Thus, 'though only Prime Minister for seven months [Law] left a decisive mark on the institutionalisation of the office by sorting out what of the Lloyd George revolution would stay and what would go' and this, Taylor believed, 'was Law's contribution as Prime Minister to British history'.[18] At the end of October Hankey sent Law a copy of *Procedure in the Cabinet Office* asking whether or not it should continue in operation. Law agreed and within a month it was if the Secretariat had never been under threat. Paradoxically for someone who wanted to return to Bagehot's PM as '*primus inter pares*', the power and authority of the office increased under Law. The Cabinet Secretariat was one element in this but others were control over a centralised party machine, disciplined parliamentary majorities, single party government, massive patronage, and the power of dissolution. Law bequeathed these resources to his successors.

The modern Conservative Party emerged in response to three developments: victory in 1918 coupled with an awareness of imperial overstretch, the threat posed by the USSR and international communism, and the extension of the franchise and rise of the Labour Party. Ramsden argues that, 'Bonar Law's real achievement as Conservative leader was to keep the party in the political game at the highest level throughout the period in which Edwardian three-party politics and then the Great War removed all certainties, to prevent any section of importance from splitting off more than temporarily, and finally to recall it to its independent identity in 1922 when the siren voices of anti-Labour coalitionism threatened to destroy both unity and coherence.'[19]

With the Coalition's destruction the final piece was in place for the Conservative Party to emerge as a mass anti-socialist party. If the modern Conservative Party emerges between 1918 and 1922 Law was not only the midwife but, by extension, its first modern leader and the country's first modern Prime Minister. Law's emphasis on tranquillity won the 1922 election but historians have concluded this was too narrow a foundation for the subsequent Conservative hegemony. Law's government hinted at a wider strategy of popular anti-socialism but Law lacked the energy or vision to exploit this opportunity despite a majority that would have kept him in office until 1927. The party lacked strategic direction and Law's version of Conservatism was an evolutionary dead end. 'It was fortunate,' Ramsden concluded, 'both for the party and for Bonar Law's reputation that this limbo did not last long ...'[20]

The loss of Conservative seats to Coalition Liberals and Labour led many Conservatives to seek independence but Law, initially, drew the opposite conclusion. This strategy was killed by the Coalition Liberal ministers in June 1920 but this did nothing to stop Labour which led directly to Law's Carlton Club speech and the Coalition's fall. Law's Carlton Club speech led to the exclusion of the Coalition ministers. Though serious, this was not a decisive split because the vast bulk of the parliamentary party and constituencies remained to provide the base for single-party, anti-socialist Conservative government. Baldwin inherited a strategic opportunity Law could not exploit. To secure Conservative hegemony Law had to go beyond negativity, the right posed no threat given his destruction of LG, his hostility to the USSR and caution over the Irish treaty but he believed there was little political space for a more socially-aware Conservatism. This was the importance of the tranquillity theme in 1922–3.

Despite his majority Law entered government in conditions of considerable personal and political uncertainty, which explains his emphasis on tone. Tone both distinguished his government from LG's and kept his (and his successor's) options open. Law's reputation was built upon the throwing of political vitriol and many feared the consequences of him behaving towards Labour he had the Liberals in 1912–14. Law, however, had changed, or at least appreciated the need to have appeared to have changed, but many remained unconvinced and this was a serious weakness. Although Law stated in public and private that he had no wish to see the Liberals replaced by Labour, he did nothing to sustain fellow anti-socialists. Law perceived a party system built around Conservative *versus* Labour was pregnant with possibilities. Thus, Cowling argues, Law's task was straightforward in conception but complex in implementation: 'The problem, then, was to govern competently and consolidate Conservative leadership of the anti-socialist forces without appearing reactionary in the process.'[21] The demands of governing exercised their own powerful logic that meant rolling back the state to the extent suggested by Law's rhetoric and preferences was not politically feasible. Law recognised such an effort would provoke a backlash that, even if defeated, would have devastating consequences; equally, protection or social reform would threaten party unity. Hence, the emphasis on tone, but this was an appeal that with Law's resignation could take the party no further. Crawford was convinced Law could not isolate his government from the new democratic dynamic; 'it is already apparent that high affirmation of principle which was to guide this government instead of the opportunism of L.G. and Co., has already been dispersed to the winds.'[22]

Law's strategy was not sustainable. Even before his resignation in May, Cabinet members were seeking a more positive Conservatism. Not temperamentally conditioned for a 'new' Conservatism, Law's image and rhetoric were dangerous for the Conservatives in a (potentially) three-party system in which a right-wing middle class backlash was a real possibility. Even though in the House he was far more emollient than before 1914, he hardly exuded an air or sympathy or empathy. In the election, for example, Law conceded that his opponents had 'shewed some very effective posters contrasting delightful rural bungalows with city slums and the comfort of the rich and the squalor of the children of the poor', but he dismissed this as typical the socialists' politics of envy.[23]

With the neutralisation of the Irish question, only tariff reform remained of Law's two political enthusiasms. His support at the Carlton Club embraced tariff reformers and free traders. Law was essentially an economic patriot, acutely conscious that fiscal policy had a proven ability to damage the party. Tariff reform became feasible only in the aftermath of the calamity of the 1929 Crash. When Law entered Number 10 he lacked, in effect, an economic policy; his object was limited to stabilisation and rolling-back the wartime state. Similarly, whilst Law wished to return to a governance less reliant on the involvement of producer groups, his rhetoric was more extreme than his actions. As PM he saw union and employer delegations and actively encouraged their engagement with ministers, and whilst the common culture and social attitudes of the industrial, commercial, bureaucratic and political elites ensured greater ease of access to business, the unions were not denied access to Whitehall.[24] From small beginnings under Law, producer group involvement, the price to be paid for governing, grew in the inter-war period, as did the state's penetration of, for example, local government. Middlemas describes Law's destruction of the Coalition and defence of party as 'a rearguard action, like Napoleon's brilliant defence of France in 1814 – a retreat, nevertheless into defeat.'[25]

In terms of foreign policy Law has been identified as one of the originators of appeasement and Law's premiership took the first steps along the path that ended on the Dunkirk beaches. The appeasement of 1922 was not that of 1938. Law's disquiet over Germany's treatment at Versailles reflected the conviction that Britain ought to encourage an equitable revision in the general interest. Britain was, after all, victorious but Law, and the political class sensed not only mass war-weariness but also signs of imperial overstretch.[26] The problems facing Britain's rivals meant, relatively speaking, Britain's 'power' had increased but that this would not last for ever as Germany would recover and Japan's power expanded in the Far East. On the horizon were the coming superpowers, the USA and USSR. Law's desire for a realistic foreign policy bringing Britain's commitment into line with its resources and defending Britain's core interests made a great deal of sense. The problem, to which Law had no answer, was the definition of these interests. This evaluation was rapidly becoming orthodox in the political and administrative elite. The road to Munich might have begun at Chanak but it was Law's successors who took that road.

Enoch Powell once commented that political careers always end in failure. Coming late to the Premiership, ill and exhausted, Bonar Law lacked the political energy, will and inspiration to implement a political vision. In any case, the world, his personal and political world, had been altered irrevocably by the war. Nonetheless, Law, in a world he neither liked nor welcomed, fatalistically did what he could to establish the 'base-line' of modern British politics and establish a governing equilibrium. Law's brief tenure means he cannot join the pantheon of great prime ministers but we should not confuse impact and importance with tenure. Premiers must be seen in their context and despite the brevity of his tenure, Law cannot, and should not, be reduced to a historical footnote.

NOTES

Chapter 1: Origins

1. H Berrington, 'Review Article. The Fiery Chariot: British Prime Ministers and the Search for Love', *British Journal of Political Science* 4 (3 July 1974) p 345.

2. R Blake, *The Unknown Prime Minister. The Life and Times of Andrew Bonar Law* (Eyre & Spottiswoode, London: 1955) p 43.

3. National Union Archives 2/1/32, p 15. Law was supporting the Liberal Unionist merger with the Conservatives (9 May 1912).

4. J Vincent (ed), *The Crawford Papers. The Journals of David Lindsay twenty-seventh Earl of Crawford and tenth Earl of Balcarres 1871–1940 during the years 1892 to 1940* (Manchester University Press, Manchester: 1984) p 263, hereafter *Crawford Papers*.

5. A J P Taylor (ed), *Lloyd George. A Diary by Francis Stevenson* (Hutchinson, London: 1971) pp 215–16, hereafter *Stevenson Diary*; P Williamson (ed), *The Modernisation of Conservative Politics. The Diaries and Letters of William Bridgeman, 1904–1935* (The Historians' Press, London: 1988) p 183, hereafter *Bridgeman Papers*; and K Middlemas (ed), *Thomas Jones' Whitehall Diary. Volume I, 1916–1925* (Oxford University Press, London: 1969) p 254, hereafter *Jones Diary*.

6. Lord Beaverbrook, *Politicians and the War 1914–1916* (Oldbourne, London: 1960) p 291.

7. J M Keynes, *The Collected Writings of John Maynard Keynes. Volume X, Essays in Biography* (Macmillan, London: 1972) p 36. Keynes's essay was written in May 1923.

8. Keynes, *Collected Writings Volume X*, p 34.

9. *Crawford Papers*, p 263.

10. *Hansard*, 28 May 1923.

11. R Rhodes James (ed), *Memoirs of a Conservative. J.C.C. Davidson's Memoirs and Papers 1910–37* (Weidenfeld & Nicolson, London: 1969) p 72.

12. Rhodes James (ed), *Memoirs of a Conservative*, p 29.

13. *Crawford Papers*, p 245.

14. *Bridgeman Papers*, p 127; and Rhodes James (ed), *Memoirs of a Conservative*, pp 27–8.

15. *Crawford Papers*, p 248.

16. R J Q Adams, *Bonar Law* (John Murray, London: 1999), p 37.

17. *Hansard*, 13 November 1923.

18. Berrington, 'Review Article: The Fiery Chariot', p 369.

19. Blake, *The Unknown Prime Minister*, p 279.

20. *Stevenson Diary*, p 106; J Barnes and D Nicholson (eds), *The Leo Amery Diaries. Volume 1: 1896–1929* (Hutchinson, London: 1980) p 234, hereafter *Amery Diaries*; and D George Boyce (ed), *The Crisis of British Unionism. The Domestic Political Papers of the Second Earl of Selbourne* (The Historians' Press, London: 1987) p 118, hereafter *Selbourne Papers*.

21. *Crawford Papers*, p 269; and *Selbourne Papers*, p 233.

22. Beaverbrook, *Politicians and the War*, pp 352–3.

23. A J P Taylor, *English History, 1914–1945* (Penguin Books, Harmondsworth: 1975) p 42.

24. Adams, *Bonar Law*, p 192.

Chapter 2: The Rise of a Good Party Man

1. Berrington, 'Review Article: The Fiery Chariot', p 363.
2. *Crawford Papers*, p 263.
3. *Amery Diaries*, p 57.
4. Rhodes James (ed), *Memoirs of a Conservative*, p 52.
5. *Crawford Papers*, p 269.
6. Blake, *The Unknown Prime Minister*, p 94; and Adams, *Bonar Law*, p 27.
7. *Crawford Papers*, p 59.
8. *Crawford Papers*, pp 146 and 160.
9. *Hansard*, 11 April 1912.
10. *Crawford Papers*, p 262.
11. *Selbourne Papers*, pp 93–4.
12. Report of the National Union Conference, November 1911, p.48. *National Union Archives 2/1/31*.
13. *Hansard*, 16 April 1912.
14. Lord Oxford and Asquith, *Memories and Reflections. Volume 1* (Cassell, London: 1928), p 239.
15. *Crawford Papers*, pp 262–3.
16. Keynes, *Collected Writings Volume X*, p 83.
17. *Hansard*, 14 February 1912.
18. Keynes, *Collected Writings Volume X*, p 83. Original emphasis.
19. *Crawford Papers*, p 238.
20. *Crawford Papers*, p 102.
21. E Halevy, *The Rule of Democracy 1905–1914* (Ernest Benn, London: 1970) p 92.
22. *Hansard*, 9 June 1909.
23. *Hansard*, 11 February 1909.
24. *Hansard*, 9 June 1909.
25. *Hansard*, 2 June 1908.
26. *Hansard*, 9 June 1909.
27. *Hansard*, 17 June 1914.

28. *Hansard*, 9 June 1909,

29. Bonar Law to Fabian Ware, 29 September 1908. *Bonar Law Papers 18/8/10*.

30. *The Times*, 26 July 1911, for Law's 'hedger' letter.

31. Report of the National Union Council for the Year 1910–1911, p 13. *National Union Archives 2/1/31*.

32. See G D Phillips, *The Diehards. Aristocratic Society and Politics in Edwardian England* (Harvard University Press, London and Cambridge, Mass: 1979) for full details.

33. *Crawford Papers*, p 237.

34. *Crawford Papers*, pp 245–6.

35. *Bridgeman Papers*, p 53.

36. V Bogdanor, 'The Selection of the Party Leader', in A Seldon and S Ball (eds), *The Conservative Century. The Conservative Party since 1900* (Oxford University Press, Oxford: 1994) p 74.

37. *Crawford Papers*, p 250.

38. *Bridgeman Papers*, p 54.

39. *Bridgeman Papers*, p 109.

40. *Crawford Papers*, p 247.

41. Rhodes James (ed), *Memoirs of a Conservative*, p 28.

42. *Crawford Papers*, p 258.

43. *Crawford Papers*, pp 247–8 and p 263.

44. *Crawford Papers*, p 258.

Chapter 3: Tariff Reform

1. *Hansard*, 22 April 1902.

2. *Hansard*, 24 November 1902.

3. *Hansard*, 12 February 1905.

4. *Hansard,* 30 March 1909.

5. *Amery Diaries*, p 92.

6. *Hansard*, 6 July 1914.

7. N Blewett, 'Free Fooders, Balfourites, Whole Hoggers. Factionalism in the Unionist Party, 1906–1910', *Historical Journal* 11 (1968) pp 95–124.

8. A Sykes, 'The Confederacy and the Purge of the Unionist Free Traders, 1906–1910', *Historical Journal* 18 (1975) pp 349–66. See also Adams, *Bonar Law*, pp 29–30.

9. *Crawford Papers*, p 122.

10. *Hansard*, 7 June 1908.

11. *Hansard*, 9 June 1909.

12. National Union Archives: National Union Conference 1911 2/1/3, pp 52–3.

13. *Crawford Papers*, p 223.

14. *Crawford Papers*, p 305.

15. *Selbourne Papers*, p 24.

16. *Crawford Papers*, pp 289–90.

17. *Crawford Papers*, p 294.

18. *Crawford Papers*, p 298.

19. *Amery Diaries*, pp 91–2.

20. *Bridgeman Papers*, p.67.

21. Bogdanor, 'The Selection of the Party Leader', p 94.

22. National Union, *Gleanings and Memoranda*, Vol. 38 (Jan-June 1912) p 161.

Chapter 4: Ulster

1. *Hansard*, 8 August 1911.

2. National Union Archives: National Union Conference 1911 *2/1/31*, p 51.

3. *Hansard*, 20 April 1911.

4. National Union Archives: National Union Conference 1911 *2/1/31*, p 48.

5. *Hansard*, 20 April 1911.

6. *Hansard*, 9 May 1911.

7. *Hansard*, 22 February 1909.

8. *Hansard*, 14 February 1912.

9. National Union, *Gleanings and Memoranda*, Vol 38 (January-June 1912) pp 1 and 6

10. National Union, *Gleanings and Memoranda* 38, p 160.

11. National Union, Gleanings *and Memoranda* 38, pp 354–9.

12. *Hansard*, 16 April 1912.

13. *Hansard*, 11 June 1912.

14. *Hansard*, 18 June 1912.

15. National Union, *Gleanings and Memoranda*, Vol 39 (July-December 1912) pp 186–7.

16. A Chamberlain, *Politics from the Inside: An Epistolary Chronicle 1906–1914* (Cassell, London: 1936) pp 486–7.

17. H Nicholson, *King George V. His Life and Reign* (Constable, London: 1952) pp 200–29.

18. National Union, *Gleanings and Memoranda*, Vol 42 (January-June 1914) pp 97–100.

19. *Hansard*, 19 March 1914.

20. J Smith, '"Paralysing the Army": The Unionists and the Army Annual Act, 1911–1914', *Parliamentary History* 15 (2) (1996) pp 191–207.

21. *Hansard*, 19 March 1914.

22. *Hansard*, 23 March 1914.

23. *Hansard*, 29 April 1914.

24. *Hansard*, 12 May 1914.

Chapter 5: War

1. A J P Taylor, 'Politics and the First World War', in *Essays in English History* (Penguin, Harmondsworth: 1976) p 242.

2. *Hansard*, 6 August 1914.

3. *Hansard*, 3 August 1914.

4. *Hansard*, 30 July 1914.

5. *Hansard*, 15 September 1914.

6. *Crawford Papers*, p 343, and *Bridgeman Papers*, p 85.

7. *Selbourne Papers*, pp 119–20.

8. S Roskill, *Hankey. Man of Secrets. Vol.1, 1877–1918* (Collins, London: 1978) p 161.

9. *Hansard*, 21 April 1915.

10. *Hansard*, 19 May 1915.

11. Rhodes James (ed), *Memoirs of a Conservative*, p 25.

12. Beaverbrook, *Politicians and the War*, pp 134–5.

13. *Amery Diaries*, p 126.

14. *Hansard*, 15 November 1915.

15. *Hansard*, 14 December 1915.

16. *Bridgeman Papers*, p 93.

17. *Hansard*, 8 November 1916. See also P J Yearwood and C Hazlehurst, 'The Affairs of a Distant Dependency: the Nigeria Debate and the Premiership, 1916', *Twentieth Century British History* 12 (4) (2001) pp 397–431.

18. *Stevenson Diary*, p 123.

19. D Lloyd George, *War Memoirs Volume 1* (Odhams Press, London: 1938) p 613.

20. Rhodes James, *Memoirs*, p 50.

21. *Selbourne Papers*, p 188.

22. *Stevenson Diary*, p 47.

23. *Hansard*, 2 May 1917.

24. *Hansard*, 22 April 1918.

25. *National Union Archives 2/1/35*. Special Conference on the Representation of the People Bill, 30 November 1917, p 5 and p 7.

26. T Wilson (ed), *The Political Diaries of C.P. Scott, 1911–28* (Collins, London: 1970) p 171, hereafter *Scott Diaries*.

27. *Stevenson Diary*, p 106, and *Scott Diaries*, p 199.

28. *Bridgeman Papers*, pp 101 and 103.

29. *National Union Archives 2/1/35*, p 7.

30. *Selbourne Papers*, pp 164–5.

31. *National Union Archives 2/1/35*, p 9.

Chapter 6: Coalition and Post-War Conservatism

1. *National Union Archives 2/1/35*, pp 14 and 15.

2. *Bridgeman Papers*, pp 140–1.

3. *Jones Diary*, p 82.

4. S Roskill, *Hankey. Man of Secrets Vol.II, 1919–1931* (Collins, London: 1972) p 120.

5. R McKibbin, *Classes and Cultures. England 1918–1951* (Oxford University Press, Oxford: 1998) p 50.

6. McKibbin, *Classes and Cultures*, p 58.

7. *Hansard,* 20 March 1919.

8. *Jones Diary*, p 101.

9. *Hansard*, 2 May 1922.

10. K O Morgan, *Consensus and Disunity: The Lloyd George Coalition 1918–1922* (Clarendon Press, Oxford: 1979) p 236.

11. National Union Conference, 10–11 June 1920, pp 34–5. *National Union Archives 2/1/36*.

12. *Selbourne Papers*, p 233.

13. National Union, *Gleanings and Memoranda* Vol 55 (January-June 1922) p 281.

14. *Hansard*, 3 April 1922.

15. *Crawford Papers*, p 410.

16. *Hansard*, 29 June 1922.

17. *Jones Diary*, p 165.

18. *Stevenson Diary*, p 235.
19. *Hansard*, 15 December 1921.
20. *The Times*, 7 October 1922.
21. Rhodes James (ed), *Memoirs of a Conservative*, p 120.
22. *Amery Diaries*, p 294, and *Bridgeman Papers*, p 160.
23. Rhodes James (ed), *Memoirs of a Conservative*, p 123.
24. Rhodes James (ed), *Memoirs of a Conservative*, p 124.
25. National Union, *Gleanings and Memoranda* Vol 56 (November 1922) pp 491–2.
26. *Amery Diaries*, p 300; *Crawford Papers*, pp 453–4; and *Bridgeman Papers*, p 161. All for 19 October 1922.
27. Rhodes James (ed), *Memoirs of a Conservative*, pp 127 and 152.
28. National Union, *Gleanings and Memoranda* 56, pp 499–500.
29. *Jones Diary*, p 220.
30. *Andrew Bonar Law's Election Address*. http://www.conservativemanifesto.com/1922. Accessed 13 July 2005. The Leader's personal election statement was the party's policy statement.
31. *NUA 2/1/35*, p 11.
32. *Jones Diary*, p 215.
33. Morgan, *Consensus and Disunity*, p 351.
34. R McKibbin, 'Class and Conventional Wisdom: the Conservative Party and the "Public" in Inter-War Britain', in *The Ideologies of Class* (Clarendon Press, Oxford: 1990) pp 281–2.
35. *Crawford Papers*, p 461.
36. National Union, *Gleanings and Memoranda* Vol 53 (Jan-June 1923) p 7.
37. *Jones Diary*, p 222.

Chapter 7: Prime Minister

1. National Union, *Gleanings and Memoranda* Vol 52 (November) 1922, p 501.
2. *Hansard*, 23 November, and 27 November 1922.
3. Roskill, *Man of Secrets Vol. II*, p 318.
4. *Hansard*, 23 November 1922.
5. *Hansard*, 13 February 1923.
6. *Hansard*, 23 November 1922.
7. *Scott Diaries*, pp 34–5.
8. Roskill, *Man of Secrets Vol. II*, p 327.
9. Rhodes James (ed), *Memoirs of a Conservative*, p 145.
10. *Hansard*, 6 March 1923.
11. *Hansard*, 2 May 1922.
12. *Hansard*, 14 December 1922.
13. *Jones Diary*, pp 225 and 227.
14. *Amery Diaries*, p 19.
15. *Bridgeman Papers*, p 164.
16. *Amery Diaries*, p 320 and Roskill, *Man of Secrets Vol. II*, p 334.
17. *Amery Diaries*, p 320.
18. *Crawford Papers*, p 465.
19. *Jones Diary,* p 228; *Amery Diaries*, p 325.

Chapter 8: Assessment

1. K Theakston and M Gill, *Rating 20th Century British Prime Ministers*. Paper to the Political Studies Association Conference, University of Leeds, 5–7 April 2005.
2. *Jones Diary*, p 233; and *Crawford Papers*, p 476.
3. *National Union Archives 2/1/35*, p 7.
4. Rhodes James (ed), *Memoirs of a Conservative*, p 51; Lloyd George, *War Memoirs Vol I*, p 605.

5. Montague-Barlow to Law, 23 April 1923. *Bonar Law Papers 111/4/22.*

6. *Hansard*, 23 November 1922.

7. *Hansard*, 28 November 1922.

8. Deputation of the TUC General Council, 16 January 1923. *Bonar Law Papers 116/3/3.*

9. Deputation from the Mineworkers Federation of Great Britain, 2 December 1922. *Bonar Law Papers 116/3/2.*

10. *Hansard*, 25 November 1922.

11. *Bonar Law Papers 116/3/2*, and Notes on a Deputation from the Railway Companies, 28 November 1922. *Bonar Law Papers 116/3/4.*

12. Deputation of the Mineworkers Federation of Great Britain, 27 February 1923. *Bonar Law Papers 117/8/6*, and National Union, *Gleanings and Memoranda* No. 57, pp 168 and 245.

13. National Union, *Gleanings and Memoranda* Vol 52 (June-December 1922) p 518.

14. *Jones Diary*, p 219.

15. Roskill, *Man of Secrets Vol II*, p 306.

16. National Union, *Gleanings and Memoranda* 52, p 518.

17. J Turner, *Lloyd George's Secretariat* (Cambridge University Press, Cambridge: 1980).

18. D Kavanagh and A Seldon, *The Powers Behind the Prime Minister. The Hidden Influence of Number Ten* (Harper Collins, London: 2000) p 47, and Taylor, *English History 1914–1945,* p 255.

19. J Ramsden, *An Appetite for Power. A History of the Conservative Party since 1830* (HarperCollins, London: 1998) p 247.

20. Ramsden, *An Appetite for Power*, p 249.

21. M Cowling, *The Impact of Labour, 1920–1924* (Cambridge University Press, Cambridge: 1971) p 245. Chapter 13 is titled 'The inadequacy of Bonar Law'.
22. *Crawford Papers*, p 476.
23. *Jones Diary*, p 222.
24. K Middlemas, *Politics in Industrial Society* (Andre Deutsch, London: 1979), especially Chapters 5 and 6.
25. Middlemas, *Politics in Industrial Society*, p 309.
26. P Kennedy, *The Realities Behind Diplomacy. Background Influences on British External Policy 1965–1980* (Fontana, London: 1981), especially Part III.

CHRONOLOGY

Year	Premiership
1922	23 October: Andrew Bonar Law becomes Prime Minister, aged 64. December: The Irish Treaty is passed by Parliament. Poincaré, Theunis and Mussolini meet with Law in London in attempt to resolve the French aggression over Germany defaulting on its war reparations.
1923	January: The delegation sent to New York to negotiate the British repayment of US war loans, including Baldwin, the Chancellor of the Exchequer, was recalled after Law refused to accept the US terms. March: The government loses three seats: Mitcham, Willesden East and Liverpool Edge Hill. April: Baldwin's budget proposes limited tax-cuts. 20 May: Bonar Law resigns, having served the shortest time of all the prime ministers of the 20th century, only 209 days. He dies five months later.

History	Culture
League of Nations council approves mandates for the former German colonies Togo, the Cameroons and Tanzania, and Palestine. British mandate proclaimed in Palestine while Arabs declare a day of mourning.	T S Eliot, *The Waste Land*. James Joyce, *Ulysses*. British Broadcasting Company (later Corporation) (BBC) founded: first radio broadcasts.
French and Belgian troops occupy the Ruhr when Germany fails to make reparation payments.	P G Wodehouse, *The Inimitable Jeeves*. George Gershwin, *Rhapsody in Blue*. BBC listings magazine *Radio Times* first published.

FURTHER READING

Law has two biographies and both are excellent. Lord Blake's *The Unknown Prime Minister: The Life and Times of Andrew Bonar Law, 1858–1923* (Eyre & Spottiswood, London: 1955) and R J Q Adams, *Bonar Law* (John Murray, London: 1999). Blake also wrote a classic general history, *The Conservative Party from Peel to Thatcher* (Fontana, London: 1985) which with John Ramsden's *An Appetite for Power. A History of the Conservative Party since 1830* (HarperCollins, London: 1998) and *The Age of Balfour and Baldwin 1902–1940* (Longmans, London: 1978) locate Law in his political and historical context. Ramsden also wrote a brief essay on Law in H Van Thal (ed), *The Prime Ministers, Volume II* (Allen and Unwin, London: 1975) and E H H Green has a perceptive essay on Law in the *Oxford Dictionary of National Biography* (2004–05).

Diaries of the period provide an insight into Law the man and his politics. Examples are, K Middlemas (ed), *Thomas Jones. Whitehall Diary Volume 1 1916–1925* (Oxford University Press, London: 1969), R Rhodes James (ed), *Memoirs of a Conservative. J.C.C. Davidson's Memoirs and Papers 1910–1937* (Weidenfeld & Nicolson, London: 1969), A J P Taylor (ed), *Lloyd George. A Diary by Francis Stevenson* (Hutchinson, London: 1971), J Barnes and D Nicholson (eds), *The Leo Amery Diaries. Volume 1: 1896–1929* (Hutchinson, London: 1980), J Ramsden (ed), *Real Old Tory Politics. The Political Diaries of Robert Sanders, Lord Bayford 1910–1935* (The Historians' Press, London: 1984), J Vincent (ed), *The Crawford Papers. The Journals of David Lindsay twenty-seventh Earl of Crawford and tenth Earl of Balcarres 1871–1940 during the years 1892 to*

1940 (Manchester University Press, Manchester: 1984), D George Boyce (ed), *The Crisis of British Unionism. The Domestic Political Papers of the Second Earl of Selbourne* (The Historians' Press, London: 1987), and P Williamson (ed), *The Modernisation of Conservative Politics. The Diaries and Letters of William Bridgeman, 1904–1935* (The Historians' Press, London: 1988). Law's relationship with Beaverbrook is covered by A J P Taylor, *Beaverbrook* (Penguin, Harmondsworth: 1972) and A Chisholm and M Davie, *Beaverbrook. A Life* (Hutchinson, London: 1992). Beaverbrook's own books such as *Men and Power 1917–1918* (Collins, London: 1956), *Politicians and the War* (Collins, London: 1960) and *The Decline and Fall of Lloyd George* (Collins, London: 1963) contain much of interest on Law.

There is a vast amount on the Edwardian Conservative Party. The best are P F Clarke's, *Lancashire and the New Liberalism* (Cambridge University Press, Cambridge: 1971), Neal Blewett, *The Peers, the Parties, and the People: The General Elections of 1910* (Macmillan, London: 1972), Alan Sykes, *Tariff Reform in British Politics 1909–1913* (Clarendon Press, Oxford: 1979), D Dutton's, *His Majesty's Loyal Opposition: The Unionist Party in Opposition 1905–1915* (Liverpool University Press, Liverpool: 1992), and E H H Green, *The Crisis of Conservatism: the Politics, Economics and Ideology of the Conservative Party, 1880–1914* (Routledge, London: 1995). The best exploration of Law's strategy over Home Rule is, J Smith, 'Bluff, Bluster and Brinkmanship: Andrew Bonar Law and the Third Home Rule Bill', *The Historical Journal* 36 (1993).

Wartime politics are explored in Cameron Hazlehurst's, *Politicians at War: July 1914 to May 1915* (Jonathan Cape, London: 1971) and John Turner's, *British Politics and the Great War: Coalition and Conflict 1915–1918* (Yale University Press, New Haven, Conn.: 1992). This also covers changing electoral behaviour, as does Kenneth D Wald's, *Crosses on the Ballot. Patterns of British Voter Alignment since 1885* (Princeton University Press, Princeton N.J.: 1983) which focuses on the rise of class politics. Specifically on Law see Martin Pugh, 'Asquith, Bonar Law, and the First Coalition', *Historical Journal* 17 (1974), Michael Fry, 'Political Change in Britain, August 1914 to December 1916', *Historical Journal* 31 (1988), Peter Yearwood and Cameron Hazlehurst, 'The Affairs of a Distant Dependency: The Nigeria Debate and the Premiership, 1916', *Twentieth Century British History* 12 (2001), and R J Q Adams, 'Andrew Bonar Law and the Fall of the Asquith Coalition: The December 1916 Cabinet Crisis', *Canadian Journal of History* 32 (1997). There is a brief essay on Law's Chancellorship in Roy Jenkins, *The Chancellors* (Macmillan, London: 1998).

Law's post-war politics are covered by Maurice Cowling, *The Impact of Labour 1920–1924: The Beginning of Modern British Politics* (Cambridge University Press, Cambridge: 1971), Michael Kinnear, *The Fall of Lloyd George: The Political Crisis of 1922* (Macmillan, London: 1973), and Kenneth Morgan, *Consensus and Disunity: The Lloyd George Coalition 1918–1922* (Clarendon Press, Oxford: 1979). For the social bases of post-war Conservatism Ross McKibbin's work is indispensable, 'Class and Conventional Wisdom: the Conservative Party and the "Public" in Inter-War Britain', in *The Ideologies of Class* (Clarendon Press, Oxford: 1990) and *Classes and Cultures. England 1918–1951* (Oxford University Press, Oxford: 1998). There is, not surprisingly, little on Law's government but useful essays are Frank Costigliola, 'Anglo-American Financial Rivalry in the 1920s', *Journal of Economic History* 37 (1977), Kevin Narizny, 'The Political Economy of Alignment. Great Britain's Commitment to Europe, 1905–39', *International Security* 27 (2003), and Elspeth O'Riordan,

'British Policy and the Ruhr Crisis 1922–24', *Diplomacy and Statecraft* 15 (2004). Keith Middlemas, *Politics in Industrial Society. The British Experience since 1911* (Andre Deutsch, London: 1979) is a magisterial survey of the changing nature of the British state under the impact of war and democracy.

PICTURE SOURCES

Page 16
Andrew Bonar Law photographed while he was Chancellor
of the Exchequer in David Lloyd George's Cabinet, circa
1916. (Courtesy Topham Picturepoint)

Page 74–5
Bonar Law photographed opening the New Colonial
Hospital at Orpington in Kent. 1916. (Courtesy Topham
Picturepoint)

Page 117
Andrew Bonar Law seen here with his sons in 1911, the
year he became leader of the Conservative Party. (Courtesy
akg Images)

INDEX